高职高专商务英语系列教材

总主编 李德荣

International Trade: Theories and Practice

主编／黎 莉

国际贸易：理论与实务

图书在版编目(CIP)数据

国际贸易：理论与实务 = International Trade: Theories and Practice / 黎莉主编. —上海：立信会计出版社，2015.7

(高职高专商务英语系列)

ISBN 978-7-5429-3667-7

Ⅰ.①国… Ⅱ.①黎… Ⅲ.①国际贸易—英语—高等职业教育—教材 Ⅳ.①H31

中国版本图书馆 CIP 数据核字(2015)第 159331 号

策划编辑　　徐雪芬　张　寻
责任编辑　　徐雪芬　周　瑜
封面设计　　周崇文

国际贸易：理论与实务

出版发行	立信会计出版社		
地　址	上海市中山西路 2230 号	邮政编码	200235
电　话	(021)64411389	传　真	(021)64411325
网　址	www.lixinaph.com	电子邮箱	lxaph@sh163.net
网上书店	www.shlx.net	电　话	(021)64411071
经　销	各地新华书店		
印　刷	常熟市梅李印刷有限公司		
开　本	787 毫米×1092 毫米	1/16	
印　张	12.5		
字　数	360 千字		
版　次	2015 年 7 月第 1 版		
印　次	2015 年 7 月第 1 次		
印　数	1—2 100		
书　号	ISBN 978-7-5429-3667-7/H		
定　价	24.00 元		

如有印订差错，请与本社联系调换

中国的企业正在转型为与国际接轨的现代企业。这一转型就宏观层面而言,是一种文化的转型。其成功与否,取决于能否借鉴世界上(尤其是发达国家和地区)已被证明为成功的企业管理文化。企业管理文化博大精深,至关重要。它大可涉及国计民生、社会安定、企业责任、管理风格,小可涉及计划安排、日常管理、服务态度、待人接物。这一文化是整个社会文化的一个重要组成部分,且直接影响人民生活。令人遗憾的是,对这一文化至今尚缺少应有的关注和倡导。

上海商贸职业教育集团根据国家经济发展战略和教育部构建现代职教体系的要求,从2009年起致力于各级各类职业教育协调发展的研究和中高职教育有效衔接的实践,完成了中高职教育定位正确、专业培养目标与职业岗位培养方向对接、学历证书与人社局职业资格证书融通的《商务英语》、《会计》、《市场营销/连锁经营管理》、《金融事务》、《国际商务》、《现代物流》、《应用艺术设计》和《酒店管理》等8个中高职教育专业教学方案。其中《商务英语》专业教学方案更是基于国际化视野、有机融入企业文化、所有课程进一步突出能力标准的全新开发。

《商务英语》专业教学方案致力于引进国际新的教育教学理念,从理论到操作层面对旧的课程设置和教学内容进行大刀阔斧的改革,使之既与国际接轨,同时适合中国国情。该教学方案大力引进国外课程,解决学英语和学专业的矛盾,意在终结英语学习和专业学习"两张皮"的历史,在探索中高职教育如何实现有效衔接或一体化的研究中取得积极的进展。项目论证的有关专家一致认为新方案从实际而非概念出发,借鉴发达国家成功经验,大胆创新,为中高职商务英语专业的发展,开创了值得努力试探和实践的新的道路。

该专业教学方案配套教材计划开发12册,这些课程包括:

The Business World(企业与社会)
Telephone Skills(电话交流技能)
Workplace Communication Skills(工作场所交流技能)
Writing Workplace Documents(工作文件写作)
Negotiation Skills(谈判技能)
How to Make a Good Presentation(演示技能)

Dealing with Customers(客户沟通技能)
Job—seeking Skills(求职技能)
International Trade Theories and Practice(国际贸易理论与实务)
Marketing Fundamentals(营销学基础)
Management Principles(管理学原理)
Basics of Financial Management(财务管理基础)

以上这些新教材以英语为载体,介绍先进的企业管理文化,同时具有语言教材的特点,更加适合中国学生学习。与传统教材相比,新教材具有下列特点。

1. 体现专业特色,迈出与国际接轨的步伐

以往的专业课程没有明确的规定和规范,各校根据自身的条件和情况开设,有的侧重外贸,有的侧重营销,也有的将重点放在开设一些单证、报关等实务课程。新教材积极借鉴国外相关经验,从培养目标出发,以"能用英语从事商务活动"为教改基本思想,以英语应用能力和商务实践能力为重点,以求达到"知识型、发展型技能人才"的培养目标。把商务专业知识的学习,与英语学习自然地融合在一起,让学生既学专业,又学英语,两者相辅相成,相得益彰。

2. 一体化设计思想指导下的中高职课程有效衔接

以往中高职教学改革互不通气,各行其是,所开设的专业课程任意性很大,重复较多,不利于专业一体化建设。新教材在中高职一体化设计思想的指导下,根据中高职商务英语专业的培养方案要求,对专业教学内容进行了有效衔接的设计,为中高职商务英语专业的课程教学提供了教学基础。新教材对课程内容和教学方法也作了明确的区分,尤其是对"双语"、"全英语"的界定,保证了中高职课程和教学内容的有效衔接。

3. 标准细化,便于操作

新教材对课程的知识和技能要求作了全新的诠释和详尽的规定,由浅入深,知行一体。在体例上,这套教材既是专业教材,又具有语言教材的特点。在介绍专业知识的同时,对专业知识的语言载体——包括词汇、句型、习惯用法、商务英语的特点等用注释、标示及各类练习等手段,让学生掌握并应用,提高英语水平。这一新的尝试,旨在努力改变以往商务英语专业存在的英语和专业"两张皮"的状况,开创一条让专业与英语融合的新路。

4. 体现先进的教学理念

新教材从内容到形式均为创新性教材,从教学内容到教学手段,既充分与国际接轨,同时适用于中国学生。为国内首创。在专业知识介绍方面,内容上力求基础、实用,文字上力求简明、通俗,以适合职业教育的特点和中高职学生现有的英语水平。

我国的职业教育与发达国家相比差距很大,这也使它具有很大的发展和创新的空间。职业教育的发展需要更多的关注、关心和扶持。本套教材系新创,问题和不足在所难免,希望广大教师在使用中提出宝贵的修改意见,以帮助本系列教材不断完善。

上海商贸职业教育集团常务副理事长冯伟国
2015年6月

中国加入世贸组织后,对我国的进出口贸易提供了更多更好的机会,同时也对开展此工作人员的岗位职业能力提出了新的要求。因此,培养熟悉国际贸易基本理论、规则和掌握从事进出口贸易实际操作技能的人才已成为当务之急。

《国际贸易理论与实务》是我国普通高等院校和高职院校商务管理、商务英语或涉外专业的一门专业课。该教材本着通俗易懂又不乏深度的原则,结合目前最新的法律、法规、惯例以及国际贸易的新形势、新特点来进行论述。本教材不论是理论部分还是实务部分,都结合了目前最新的理论动向和大量的实际案例。

本教材分为两大部分:第一部分的主要内容是国家之间为何贸易;第二部分的主要内容是国家之间如何贸易。

在第一部分,教材介绍了国际贸易的理论知识,主要包括国际贸易的基本贸易理论,并对国际惯例进行了原则性的简要论述,包括国际贸易政策和国际贸易术语等。

本教材在内容上更注重实务环节,这体现在教材的第二部分。在这一部分中,教材力求将国际贸易中从国际贸易操作程序、商品的交易条款、国际货运与保险、付款方式及检验、索赔、不可抗力与仲裁等最常用、最基本的实用操作过程——进行介绍。

本教材具有以下特点:

1. 结合商务英语专业对语言有较高要求的特点,用英语进行教材的编写。但是,我们还必须考虑高职学生的学习能力、认知水平等特点,因此在教材的内容编写上,通常采用简单易懂的语言表达方式,同时大量的国际贸易中各个环节的操作实例,让学生能够通过深入浅出的方式,比较轻松地理解所学课程内容。

2. 图文并茂的专业练习和语言训练是本教材的又一个亮点。它结合本单元学习的知识和内容,在帮助学生理解和巩固课程内容的同时,能让学生在使用语言完成工作任务的过程中提高语言能力,起到一举两得的作用。

3. 为了让学生具备实际的操作能力,根据每个章节及主要内容,我们安排了一连串的"Case Study"。这样能让学生在学完一个单元后,有机会就国际贸易中的某个环节进行实践操作,从而提高高职学生的实践操作能力。

本教材由上海工商职业技术学院黎莉老师主编,参加编写的有朱佳敏和徐毓雯老师。在编写过程中,编者查阅了大量的国内外资料,同时向企业的诸多业内行家进行咨询和请教,在此向各位表示衷心的感谢。

为方便教学,本书配有习题参考答案,需要的读者可访问 www.lixinaph.com 获取。

由于编者水平有限,书中缺点、疏漏或不妥之处在所难免,欢迎使用本教材的老师和同学多多指点批评,提出宝贵意见,使之完善。

编　者
2015 年 6 月

Contents

Chapter 1 International Trade Theory and Development ········· 1
1. A General Introduction to International Trade ········· 1
2. Basic Theories of International Trade ········· 9
3. World Trading System and Regional Economic Integration ········· 18

Chapter 2 International Trade Policy ········· 26
1. Tariff Barriers ········· 26
2. Non-tariff Barriers ········· 32
3. Other Trade Policies ········· 37

Chapter 3 Trade Terms and Pricing ········· 45
1. International Trade Terms ········· 45
2. Pricing ········· 52

Chapter 4 International Trade Procedure ········· 59
1. Launching a Profitable Transaction ········· 59
2. Business Negotiation and Trade Contract ········· 66
3. Performance of the Contract ········· 74

Chapter 5 Commodity Terms in International Trade ········· 83
1. Name of Commodity ········· 83
2. Quality of Commodity ········· 90
3. Quantity of Commodity ········· 99
4. Packing and Marking of Commodity ········· 106

Chapter 6　International Cargo Transportation and Insurance ········· 116
1. Ocean Transportation ··· 116
2. Other Modes of Transportation ·· 123
3. Shipment Clause, Bill of Lading ·· 129
4. International Cargo Transportation Insurance ······································ 137

Chapter 7　International Payment ··· 142
1. Paying Instrument ··· 142
2. Payment Methods ··· 149
3. Payment Methods of Letter of Credit ·· 154

Chapter 8　Inspection, Claim, Force Majeure and Arbitration ············· 162
1. Commodity Inspection ·· 162
2. Claim ··· 169
3. Force Majeure ·· 176
4. Arbitration ·· 183

Chapter 1

International Trade Theory and Development

1. A General Introduction to International Trade

International trade[1], as its name implies, refers to the exchange activities of goods and services between nations. It has several forms, such as "*foreign trade*[2]" and "*overseas trade*[3]", of which the former *stands for*[4] global trade of a single nation with others, and the latter is usually regarded as the trade between island countries and outside world.

International trade takes place for many reasons. The first is that no nation has all of the commodities that it needs, because raw materials are scattered around the world and countries which do not have the resources within their own boundaries must buy from others. Second, for most countries, international trade is an essential part of economy. The ratio of dependence on foreign trade is the rate of the *total value of foreign trade*[5] in the *Gross Domestic Product (GDP)*[6] or *Gross National Product (GNP)*[7]. It shows how heavy the international trade weighs in national economy. Besides, it is also a common *indicator*[8] of to what extent a nation participates in the *international division of labor*[9].

Another system to evaluate the situation of foreign trade is the *balance of trade*[10]. The balance of trade is the difference between the monetary value of exports and imports of a country over a certain period. A positive balance is known as a *trade surplus*[11], or a *favorable balance of trade*[12], if export exceeds import; the *opposite scenario*[13] is referred to as a *trade deficit*[14], or an *unfavorable balance of trade*[15]. Balance of trade is the largest component of a country's *balance of payments*[16], it is sometimes divided into a goods and a services balance.

The Classification of International Trade

To begin the research of this subject, we should basically recognize the classification of international trade.

◇ By movement of goods and services

- Export. It is the process of selling and shipping the goods and services produced in the home country to overseas markets.
- Import. This activity involves buying goods and services from other countries, and then selling them in local market.
- *Entrepot trade*[17]. For many reasons, the final import country could not deal with the export country directly, but through a third country, trade in this kind is called entrepot trade. *The imported goods are re-exported with or without any additional processing or repackaging*[18].
- *Transit trade*[19]. Shipment of the foreign goods should go through a third country or more to reach the destination. It should be noted that shipment by air across the third nation's *airspace*[20] is excluded from transit trade.
- Re-Export trade. This kind of foreign trade means exports of foreign goods in the same state as previously imported. It is closely related to Entrepot Trade.
- Re-Import trade. Normally, re-import trade is caused by *return of goods*[21] or other incidental reasons.

◇ By property of trade objects

From the definition of international trade, we get to know that it mainly includes two species of transaction objects: the *tangible*[22] goods and intangible services.

The Apple Inc. products greeted by *all strata*[23], the Chanel cosmetics used to makeup ladies, the Ferrari running in the highway and the Mitsubishi elevator in the mansion and shopping malls, all of these are physically tangible and visible. The import and export of such goods is the so-called *visible trade*[24]. Because *customs clearance*[25] is required in visible trade, the trade value will be included into *customs statistic*[26] and thus constitutes a nation's total value of foreign trade over a certain period.

And thanks to *invisible trade*[27], Chinese audience can watch the latest season of "Sherlock Holmes" in Youku.com, tourists can use credit cards to pay bills when travelling overseas, and the patent claim between Samsung and Apple provides us lots of topics. Invisible trade is, though intangible and unable to be calculated by customs, a dominant part of a nation's balance of payments. It mainly includes international exchange of services and techniques.

◇ By trade policy

On the basis of trade policy, international trade could also be *categorized*[28] as *free* trade[29] and *protective trade*[30].

Unlike individuals and families, or other small units of trade participants, nations act differently in trade with their *counterparts*[31]. Being *sovereign*[32], a nation can use policy tools to set all sorts of barriers between its residents and outside world. But meanwhile, it makes every effort, by policy or other measures, to push the outflow of its products and factors. That is protective trade.

Conversely, free trade is a policy by which governments neither facilitate nor pose obstacles to import and export[33]. That means the *circulation*[34] of goods and services worldwide is absolutely *unrestricted*[35], no tariff, no duties and no *quota*[36] at all. The open market *functions*[37] and nations compete freely in the world market.

International Trade Is Important

Before we further learn this subject, it is beneficial to have a look at some basic trade statistics to give us a sense of the importance of international trade.

Figure 1-1 shows the growth trend of China's GDP and the annual total value of foreign trade from 2002 to 2012. The most obvious feature of the figure is the long-term upward trend in both GDP and total value of foreign trade: both of them have risen almost *fivefold*[38] in volume. As one of the key sector of China's economy, export has contributed a noticeable part to the boost of GDP.

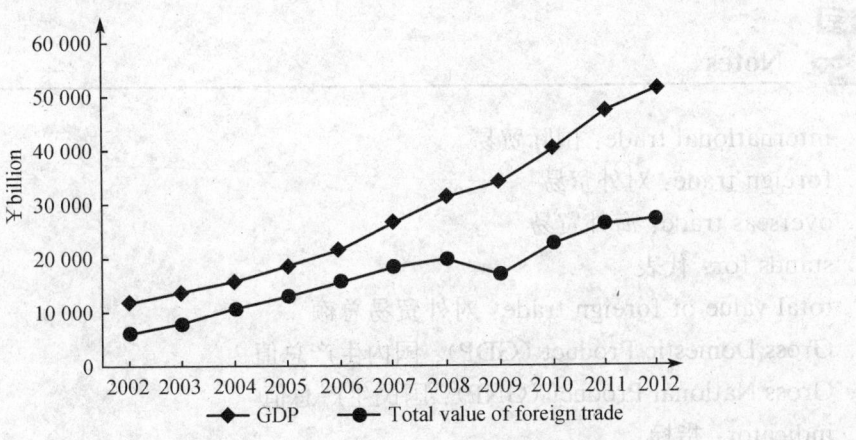

Figure 1-1 China's GDP and Total Value of Foreign Trade

How important is international trade in the economies of various countries? The Table 1-1 examines one measure of the importance of trade to a country. The ratio of the sum of a country's total trade to the country's GDP. Though the indicators are not so comparable, yet they provide a reasonable way of comparing the importance of trade across time and across countries.

Here are some observations about what we see in the table. First, for each of the countries listed in the table (also for those unlisted), international trade has become more important as the result of globalization. Second, developing countries like China and India have become much more dependent on international trade in the past several decades. That is mainly because these countries finally opened up to free trade.

Table 1-1 Exports Plus Imports as a Percentage of GDP

	1970	2009
Australia	25.8	40.3
Canada	42.0	59.1
China	5.3	47.1
France	31.1	48.0
India	8.0	45.8
Japan	20.3	24.8
Korea	37.7	95.9
United Kingdom	43.6	57.8
Unite States	11.1	25.1

Notes

1. international trade：国际贸易
2. foreign trade：对外贸易
3. overseas trade：海外贸易
4. stands for：代表
5. total value of foreign trade：对外贸易总额
6. Gross Domestic Product (GDP)：国内生产总值
7. Gross National Product (GNP)：国民生产总值
8. indicator：指标
9. international division of labor：国际分工
10. balance of trade：贸易差额
11. trade surplus：贸易盈余；出超
12. favorable balance of trade：贸易顺差
13. opposite scenario：相反的情形

Chapter 1
International Trade Theory and Development

14. trade deficit：贸易赤字；入超
15. unfavorable balance of trade：贸易逆差
16. balance of payments：国际收支差额
17. entrepot trade：转口贸易
18. The imported goods are re-exported with or without any additional processing or repackaging：进口的商品经过或未经过加工或再包装销往国外
19. transit trade：过境贸易
20. airspace：领空
21. return of goods：退货
22. tangible：可触摸的，实体的
23. all strata：各个阶层
24. visible trade：有形贸易
25. customs clearance：清关
26. customs statistic：海关统计
27. invisible trade：无形贸易
28. categorized：把……归类为
29. free trade：自由贸易
30. protective trade：保护贸易
31. counterparts：同类
32. sovereign：具有独立主权的
33. Conversely, free trade is policy by which governments neither facilitate nor pose obstacles to import and export：相反，自由贸易即政府对进出口既不给予便利也不设置障碍的政策
34. circulation：流通
35. unrestricted：不受限制的
36. quota：限额
37. functions：行使职能
38. fivefold：五倍

In Practice

> ## Questions Based on the Text

I. Decide whether the following statements are true or false according to the text.

1. International trade is totally different from foreign trade.　　　　　　　　( )

2. The rate of import price in export price is the dependence of foreign trade. (   )
3. In any case, trade surplus is better than trade deficit. (   )
4. From the definition of international trade, we get to know that it mainly includes two species of transaction objects: the tangible goods and intangible services. (   )
5. Copyright is included in visible goods. (   )
6. Conversely, free trade is policy by which governments neither facilitate nor pose obstacles to import and export. (   )
7. On the basis of trade policy, international trade could also be categorized as free trade and protective trade. (   )
8. In China, export has contributed a noticeable part to the boost of GDP. (   )

II. Answer these questions according to the text.
1. What is international trade?
2. For most countries, is international trade an essential part of economy? Why?
3. What are the classifications of international trade?
4. What's the difference between visible trade and invisible trade?
5. Why some developing countries have become more dependent on international trade in the past several decades?

> **Business Vocabulary and Useful Expressions**

III. Translate the following terms.
1. invisible trade _____
2. trade deficit _____
3. industrial free zone _____
4. customs clearance _____
5. return of goods _____
6. international division of labor _____
7. 贸易差额 _____
8. 保护贸易 _____
9. 专门贸易 _____
10. 海外贸易 _____
11. 海关统计 _____
12. 国际收支差额 _____

Chapter 1
International Trade Theory and Development

IV. Fill in the blanks with words or phrases given below. Change the form where necessary.

> global   essential   ratio   indicator   evaluate

1. The _____ view, the ability to make wider decisions based on a knowledge of all the facts, not just some of them.
2. ...vital economic _____, such as inflation, growth and the trade gap.
3. The bottom chart shows the _____ of personal debt to personal income.
4. The market situation is difficult to _____.
5. Jordan promised to trim the city budget without cutting _____ services.

> deficit   classification   intangible   counterpart   circulation

6. Its tariffs cater for four basic _____ of customer.
7. The organization was very different from that of its _____ in the rest of the Nordic region.
8. The supply of money in _____ was drastically reduced overnight.
9. There are _____ benefits beyond a rise in the share price.
10. They're ready to cut the federal budget _____ for the next fiscal year.

> refers to   stand for   exclude from   be divided into   all sorts of

11. The possibility of total loss can be _____ our calculations.
12. All things invariably _____ two.
13. What does EU _____?
14. The bank staff got up to _____ antics to raise money for charity.
15. What I have to say _____ all of you.

V. Look at the commodity pictures below and choose the right answer.

Online games	1. Trade of operation rights of online games belongs to _____. a. visible trade b. invisible trade
Personal computers	2. Trade of personal computers belongs to _____. a. visible trade b. invisible trade

(Continued)

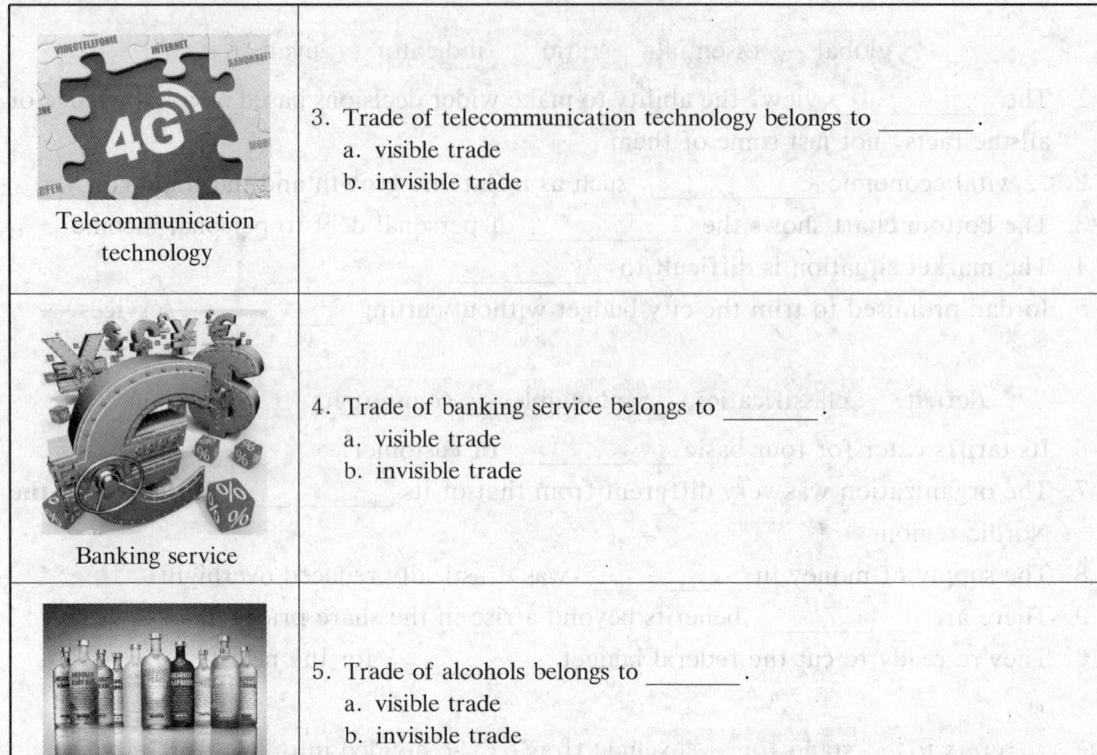

Telecommunication technology	3. Trade of telecommunication technology belongs to _____.
	  a. visible trade
	  b. invisible trade

Banking service	4. Trade of banking service belongs to _____.
	  a. visible trade
	  b. invisible trade

Alcohols	5. Trade of alcohols belongs to _____.
	  a. visible trade
	  b. invisible trade

➢ Case Study

International markets were of growing significance to the U. S. film and television business. Hollywood was also important to the U. S. economy; by 1991, the film and television industry generated an annual trade surplus of more than $4.5 billion, second only to the aerospace business.

"Keep in mind," remarked Jack Valenti, the president of the Motion Picture Association of America, "that the U. S. film industry does about $24 billion a year. Forty-one percent of that comes from international markets, so it is increasingly crucial and important that those markets remain open."

What does this article indicate? Which is more important in international trade, the visible trade or the invisible trade?

2. Basic Theories of International Trade

Imagine we are living in a world with no international trade at all and think of what products you could buy in the market and how much you need to pay for a certain product.

In China, millions of workers would lose their jobs in *manufacturing industry*[1] because no orders would be placed by foreign companies any more. And Americans, some might be happy because they could get a job due to the huge *labor demand*[2], but most would probably suffer from an *increasing level of inflation*[3]. Japanese, however, might face a more difficult situation than its *counterparts*[4], since the majority of resources they need to keep the operation of their society come from overseas. It is not difficult to imagine that similar *scenarios*[5] would unfold in other countries.

All in all, even the world without international trade would not *get into a mess*[6], but certainly it can't turn out to be as good as the real one we are living in. As for this reason, we should start the story from why international trade occurs.

Mercantilism[7]

As the first *school*[8] of economic thought about international trade, mercantilism appeared in the 15th century and dominated West Europeans' thinking of wealth several centuries after its birth. It cannot be classified as *a formal system of thought*[9], but rather as *a collection of similar attitudes toward domestic economic activity*[10].

One of the *central beliefs*[11] of mercantilism was that *national well-being*[12] or wealth was based on national holdings of precious metals such as gold and silver. The question is: where do the gold and silver come from? Besides mining *the limited reserves*[13], foreign exchange of goods and precious metals seems to be the only choice.

Another popular thought of Mercantilism was the *static*[14] view of world resources. Due to this belief, international trade was regarded as a *zero-sum game*[15] in which one country's gain was at the expense of another. Thus, mercantilist reviewed exports were good and imports were bad.

The goal of policies made by dominators during this period was *to ensure a trade surplus and a net inflow of money*[16]. These policies include:

- Government controlled the transaction and use of precious metals.
- Government prohibited the export of precious metals by individuals. *Individuals caught smuggling specie were subject to severe punishment, often death*[17].
- Exports were *subsidized*[18] but high tariffs and quotas were imposed on imports.

Frederick Engelsonce drew a vivid analogy between misers and European countries which carried out mercantilism[19], in his outlines of a critique of Political Economy:

The nations faced each other like misers, each clasping to himself with both arms his precious money-bag, eyeing his neighbors with envy and distrust. [20]

History has proved that Mercantilism finally became a cause of frequent European wars in that time and motivated colonial expansion.

Adam Smith's Theory of Absolute Advantage

In Europe, academic belief in mercantilism began to fade in the late 18th century, especially in Britain, *in light of*[21] the arguments of Adam Smith and the classical economists. In the late 18th and early 19th centuries, first Adam Smith and David Ricardo explored the basis for international trade as part of their effort to make a case for free trade.

In his *Wealth of Nations*, Adam Smith compared nations to household. He wrote:

It is the maxim of every prudent master of a family, never to attempt to make at home what it will cost... more to make than to buy. The tailor does not attempt to make his own shoes, but buys them from the shoemaker...

If a foreign country can supply us with a commodity cheaper than we ourselves can make it, better buy it of them with some part of the product of our own industry, employed in a way in which we have some advantage.

Adam Smith noticed the difference in productivity in making the same products between different countries, owing to the skills of their workers or the quality of their natural resources. He termed the superiority in productivity "absolute advantage". An example will be used to illustrate this theory. *Provided that*[22] only two countries in the world, China and the rest. And the two products are cloth and wine. To simplify, we consider the only resource used to produce both products are labor. Here labor presents a bundle of resources used to produce the real products. Suppose that China is better at producing cloth, and the rest of the world is better at producing wine.

As Table 1-2 shows, *the labor productivity*[23] of China in cloth is higher than the rest of the world, in another word, China has an *absolute advantage*[24] in producing cloth. Similarly, the rest of the world has an advantage in producing wine. If it is not possible to trade between these two countries, then each country will have to produce both of the products domestically to satisfy its demand. If international trade is permitted, then China can focus on producing cloth but import wine from the rest of the world *and vice versa*[25]. The result is total production of the world increases.

Table 1-2

	Country	Units of cloth	Labor hours	Units of wine	Labor hours
before division	China	1	60	1	120
	the rest	1	100	1	80
after division	China	3	180		
	the rest			2.25	180
after exchange	China	1		2	
	the rest	1.25		1	

Adam Smith's theory illuminates international trade is not a zero-sum activity. In most cases, both countries will benefit from trade by splitting the benefits of the enhanced world production. However, if a country has no absolute advantage, will it be hurt by international trade? Adam Smith's theory obviously fails to answer this realistic question.

David Ricardo's Theory of Comparative Advantage

The main contribution of David Ricardo's theory was to show that even a country has no absolute advantage at all can benefit from international trade. In the early 19th century, Ricardo demonstrated the principle of *comparative advantage*[26] in his writing: A country will export the goods and services that it can produce at a low *opportunity cost*[27] and import the goods and services that it would otherwise produce at a high opportunity cost. The key word "comparative" refers to "relative" and "not necessarily absolute". And the opportunity cost here means to give up the amount of production of one product in order to produce the other product by shifting production resources from one to the other.

The example used here to illustrate Ricardo's theory is similar to Adam Smith's but with a few changes in the assumptions. Suppose China has an absolute advantage in producing both cloth and wine, and the rest of the world has absolute disadvantage. Table 1-3 shows the result if China focuses on producing cloth in which it has the greatest relative advantage but imports wine while the rest of the world does the opposite. Each country can *benefit from*[28] trade by exporting products in which it has the greatest relative advantage (or least relative disadvantage) and importing products in which it has the least relative advantage (or the greatest relative disadvantage).

The result manifests that it is the comparative advantage not the absolute advantage that drives the trade between two countries. The world economy arises basically as well and the world people have more to consume actually.

Table 1-3

	Country	Units of cloth	Labor hours	Units of wine	Labor hours
before division	China	1	80	1	90
	the rest	1	120	1	100
after division	China	2.125	170		
	the rest			2.2	220
after exchange	China	1		1.125	
	the rest	1.2		1	

However, the comparative advantage theory was also attacked by many economists because it was pointed out that the theory was built on some unrealistic assumptions such as no transportation costs, no differences in the prices of resources, no tariffs or other trade barriers and so on.

Heckscher-Ohlin Theory of *Factor Endowment*[29]

To Ricardo, labor was the only factor of production, therefore comparative advantage could arise only due to international differences in labor productivity. In the real world, however, while trade is partly explained by differences in labor productivity, it also reflects differences in countries' resources. Australia exports *iron ores*[30] to China not because its miners are more productive relative to their China counterparts but because sparsely populated Australia has more iron mines *per capita*[31] than China. Thus a realistic view of trade must allow for the importance not just of labor, but also of other factors of production such as land, capital, and mineral resources.

That international trade is largely driven by differences in countries' resources which is one of the most *influential*[32] theories in international economics. Developed by two Swedish economists, Eli Heckscher(1919) and Bertil Ohlin (1933), the theory is often referred to as the Heckscher-Ohlin theory. Because the theory emphasizes the *interplay*[33] between the proportions in which different factors of production are available in different countries and the proportions in which they are used in producing different goods, it is also referred to as the *factor-proportions theory*[34].

In the more realistic case with multiple countries, factors of production, and numbers of goods, we can generalize this theory as a correlation between a country's abundance in a factor and its exports of goods that use that factor intensively: *Countries tend to export goods whose production is intensive in factors with which the countries are abundantly endowed*[35]. To put it simply, a capital abundant country will export *capital intensive*[36] goods, while a labor abundant country will export *labor intensive*[37] goods.

Notes

1. manufacturing industry：制造业
2. labor demand：劳动力需求
3. increasing level of inflation：日益增长的通货膨胀水平
4. counterparts：与对方地位相当的人或物，此处指其他国家
5. scenarios：情形
6. get into a mess：陷入困境
7. mercantilism：重商主义
8. school：流派
9. a formal system of thought：一个正式的思想体系
10. a collection of similar attitudes toward domestic economic activity：对国内经济活动的一系列相似观点的集合
11. central beliefs：中心思想
12. national well-being：国民财富
13. the limited reserves：有限的储量
14. static：静态的，静止的
15. zero-sum game：零和竞赛，零和游戏
16. to ensure a trade surplus and a net inflow：确保贸易顺差和入超净额
17. Individuals caught smuggling specie were subject to severe punishment, often death：偷运金币的个人一旦被抓会被判以重罪，往往是死刑
18. subsidized：以津贴补助
19. Frederick Engels once drew a vivid analogy between misers and European countries which carried out mercantilism：弗里德里希·恩格斯曾经将实行重商主义的欧洲国家生动地比喻为吝啬鬼
20. The nations faced each other like misers, each clasping to himself with both arms his precious money-bag, eyeing his neighbors with envy and distrust：这些国家就像守财奴一样，双手抱住自己心爱的钱袋，用妒嫉猜疑的眼光打量着自己的邻居
21. in light of：根据
22. provided that：假设

23. the labor productivity：劳动生产率
24. absolute advantage：绝对优势
25. and vice versa：反之亦然
26. comparative advantage：比较优势
27. opportunity cost：机会成本
28. benefit from：受益于
29. factor endowment：要素禀赋
30. iron ores：铁矿石
31. per capita：人均
32. influential：有影响力的
33. interplay：相互作用
34. factor-proportions theory：要素比例理论
35. Countries tend to export goods whose production is intensive in factors with which the countries are abundantly endowed：国家倾向于出口密集的、使用本国丰富资源生产出来的产品
36. capital intensive：资本密集型
37. labor intensive：劳动密集型

In Practice

Questions Based on the Text

I. Decide whether the following statements are true or false according to the text.

1. The majority of resources Japanese needs to consume are imported from overseas. (   )
2. These mercantilist reviewed exports were bad and imports were good. (   )
3. Absolute advantage is the absolute inferiority in efficiency. (   )
4. David Ricardo found even a country which has no absolute advantage at all can benefit from international trade. (   )
5. That international trade is largely driven by differences in countries' resources which is one of the most influential theories in international economics. (   )

II. Answer these questions according to the text.

1. What is the central belief of mercantilism about national well-being?
2. What does the static view of resources refer to?

3. How to evaluate Adam Smith's theory of absolute advantage?
4. What was the main contribution of David Ricardo's theory?
5. What is the principle of factor proportion theory?

➤ **Business Vocabulary and Useful Expressions**

III. Translate the following terms.
1. allow for _____
2. absolute advantage _____
3. in most cases _____
4. benefit from _____
5. get into a mess _____
6. zero-sum game _____
7. 贵金属 _____
8. 机会成本 _____
9. 重商主义 _____
10. 比较优势 _____
11. 资本密集型 _____
12. 要素禀赋 _____

IV. Fill in the blanks with words or phrases given below. Change the form where necessary.

| illustrate | simplify | illuminate | enhance | contribution |

1. Our interesting teacher could _____ almost any subject we studied.
2. The growth of a city often _____ the value of land close to it.
3. The guide is _____ with full-colour photographs.
4. They _____ the way we pay taxes.
5. All _____, however small, will be greatly appreciated.

| demonstrate | reflect | emphasize | interplay | available |

6. Most of us know the _____ between inheritance and learning.
7. The season ticket is _____ for three months.
8. Our study _____ beyond doubt that the play was written by Shakespeare.
9. Shares are priced at a level that _____ a company's prospects.
10. I must _____ that this is only a summary, and the full report will not be available until next week.

| focus on | mean...to | due to | relative to | refer to |

11. Unemployment _____ automation will grow steadily.
12. Many firms are _____ increasing their markets overseas.
13. _____ the dictionary when you don't know how to spell a word.
14. These symbols _____ nothing _____ me.
15. If you have any queries _____ payment, please contact us.

➢ Workshop

V. Put these three names into the correct place in the table.

| a. Adam Smith | b. David Ricardo | c. Eli Heckscher |

Founder's Name	Theory
i	comparative advantage
ii	factor endowment
iii	absolute advantage

VI. Look at the commodity pictures below and choose the right answer.

Real estate	1. Real estate is a _____ industry.
	  a. capital intensive
	  b. labor intensive

Banking	2. Banking is a _____ industry.
	  a. capital intensive
	  b. labor intensive

(Continued)

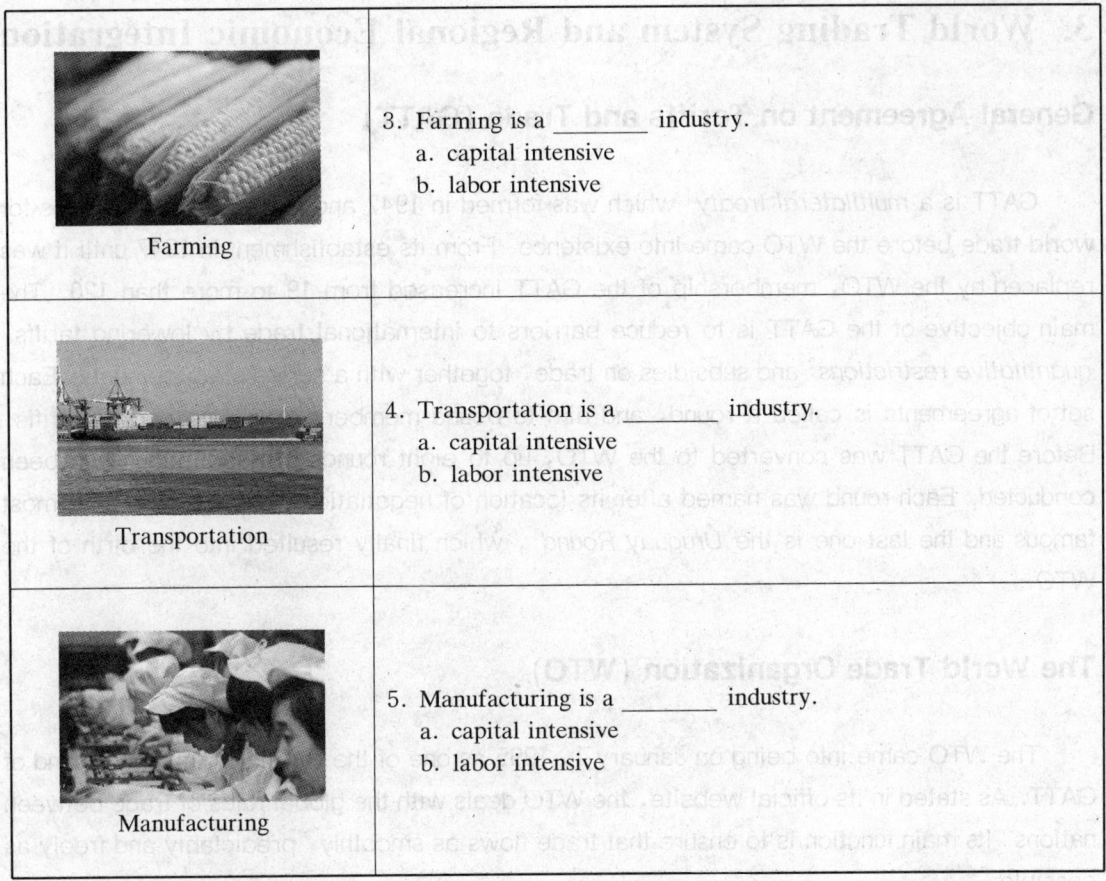

3. Farming is a _____ industry.
   a. capital intensive
   b. labor intensive

4. Transportation is a _____ industry.
   a. capital intensive
   b. labor intensive

5. Manufacturing is a _____ industry.
   a. capital intensive
   b. labor intensive

➤ **Case Study**

If you are reading this while fully clothed, the odds are that crucial parts of your outfit came from the Chinese town of Qiaotou, which produces 60 percent of the world's buttons and a large proportion of its zippers, too.

Qiaotou isn't unique. "In China, many small towns, not even worthy of a speck on most maps, have also become world-beaters by focusing on labour-intensive niches... Start at the toothbrush town of Hangji, pass the tie mecca of Shengzhou, head east to the home of cheap cigarette lighters in Zhang Qi, slip down the coast to the giant shoe factories of Wen Ling, then move back inland to Yiwu, which not only makes more socks than anywhere else on earth, but also sells almost everything under the sun."

What facts can we get from the passage above?

3. World Trading System and Regional Economic Integration

General Agreement on Tariffs and Trade (GATT)

GATT is a *multilateral treaty*[1] which was formed in 1947 and had provided the rules for world trade before the WTO came into existence. From its establishment in 1947 until it was replaced by the WTO, membership of the GATT increased from 19 to more than 120. The main objective of the GATT is to reduce barriers to international trade by lowering tariffs, *quantitative restrictions*[2] and subsidies on trade, together with a series of agreements. Each set of agreements is called a round, and aim to bound members to reduce certain tariffs. Before the GATT was converted to the WTO, up to eight rounds of negotiations had been conducted. Each round was named after its location of negotiation. Among them, the most famous and the last one is the *Uruguay Round*[3], which finally resulted into the birth of the WTO.

The World Trade Organization (WTO)

The WTO came into being on January 1, 1995 as one of the results of Uruguay Round of GATT. As stated in its official website, the WTO deals with the global rules of trade between nations. Its main function is to ensure that trade flows as smoothly, predictably and freely as possible.

The WTO is run by its member governments. All major decisions are made by the membership as a whole, either by ministers (who usually meet at least once every two years) or by their ambassadors or delegates (who meet regularly in Geneva).

◇ The fundamental principles of the WTO

The WTO agreements cover a wide variety of aspects, such as agriculture, textiles and clothing, banking, telecommunications, government purchases, industrial standards and product safety, *food sanitation*[4], intellectual property, and so on. All of these activities are run under a series of fundamental principles. These principles are the foundation of the multinational trading system.
- Trade without discrimination, including *most-favored-nation treatment*[5] (MFNT) and *national treatment*[6].
- Free trade: gradually, through negotiation.

- Predictability: through *binding and transparency*[7].
- Promoting fair competition.
- Encouraging development and economic reform.

For detailed version of these principles, please refer to http://www.wto.org/.

◇ China and the WTO

Though China was one of the 23 original signatories of the GATT, China experienced a long and rough way to enter the WTO. After eight-years continuous effort to return to GATT and six-years negotiation with all the existent members of the WTO, China was finally accepted as the 143th member of the WTO on December 11, 2001.

Thirteen years after accession, China has smoothly gone through the *transition period*[8], and achieved remarkable gains. To date, China has become the world's second largest economy as measured by GDP, forwarded 5 ranks compared to its ranking in 2000. Meanwhile, the total value of foreign trade increased from $509.65 billion in 2001 to $2.97 trillion in 2010, ranked first in exporting and second in importing worldwide. Figure 1-2 illustrates the increasing trend of China's annual foreign trade volume.

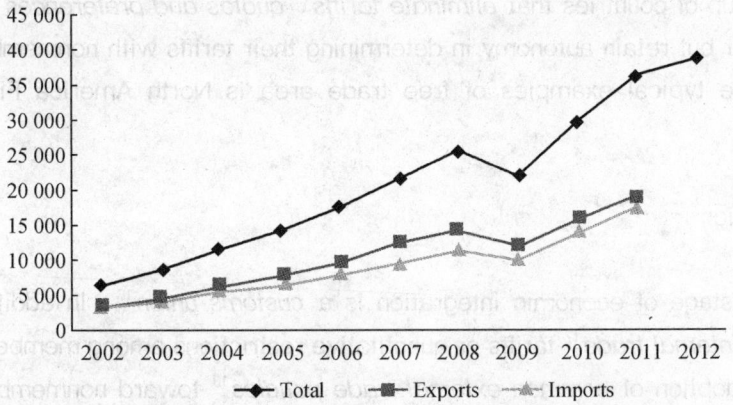

Figure 1-2 China's annual statistics of imports and exports

Regional Economic Integration

Regional economic integration[9] refers to a process in which countries enter into a regional agreement with the view of enhancing regional economic cooperation through regional institutions and rules. The main aims of regional economic integration include reducing, and ultimately removing, tariff and *non-tariff barriers*[10] to free flow of goods, services, and factors of production among countries.

Regional trading blocs[11] differ significantly in form and function. The degree of economic integration can be classified into six stages as follows.

◇ Preferential trade agreement

Preferential trade agreement[12], also called PTA, is the least restrictive and loosest form of regional economic integration. Members who signed the agreement grant preferential *access to*[13] certain products from other members by reducing tariffs, but not by getting rid of them completely. On the other hand, they *retain tariff protection*[14] on goods entering their market from non-members.

Asia-Pacific Trade Agreement (APTA), signed in 1975, is the oldest preferential trade agreement between developing countries in the Asia-Pacific region.

◇ Free trade area

A Free trade area, which can be regarded as the second stage of economic integration, refers to a group of countries that *eliminate tariffs, quotas and preferences*[15] on most trade with each other but retain autonomy in determining their tariffs with nonmembers.

One of the typical examples of free trade area is North America Free Trade Area (NAFTA).

◇ Customs union

The third stage of economic integration is a *customs union*[16]. In addition to the total elimination of *internal trade*[17] tariffs or quantitative restrictions among member states, it also involves the adoption of *common external trade policies*[18] toward nonmembers. Typically, this takes the form of a common external tariff, whereby imports from non-members are subject to the same tariff when sold to any member country.

Some current customs unions that have come into force are as follows:
- Arab Customs Union (ACU)
- Closer Economic Relations (CER between Australia and New Zealand)

◇ Common market

Common market is a further step of customs union. A common market eliminates all *barriers to trade*[19] among members and formulates a common external trade policy. In addition, it removes all the barriers that hinder the free movement of factors of production among member states, such as physical borders, technical standards and *fiscal taxes*[20].

Factors of production include capital, labor and technology. In a common market, an individual can be employed by a corporation located in any member state of common market; capital can flow to where it can earn *the highest remuneration*[21]; business can be extended into any of the participating states.

An example of common market is the *European Community（EC）*[22], which officially began on January 1, 1958, and later became *the European Union（EU）*[23].

◇ Economic union

As the fifth stage of economic integration, an economic union is also called an *economic and monetary union*[24]. The "economic" aspect of economic union refers to the existence of a common market, and the "monetary" aspect refers to the introduction of a common currency in cooperation with *highly unified*[25] fiscal policies.

The most famous example of this form is the EU, which is established on November 1, 1993.

◇ Complete economic integration

The highest level of economic integration is known as complete economic integration, which represents full integration of the economies of two or more countries. A complete economic integration requires its members to carry out thoroughly unified economic and social policies, involving monetary policy, fiscal policy, taxation, and regional development policy, etc., in order to blend their economies into a single unity.

At present, only the EU is making efforts to achieve the goal of being a complete economic integration, although not so smoothly.

Notes

1. multilateral treaty：多边条约
2. quantitative restrictions：数量管制
3. Uruguay Round：乌拉圭回合
4. food sanitation：食品卫生
5. most-favored-nation treatment：最惠国待遇

6. national treatment：国民待遇
7. through binding and transparency：通过约束力和透明度原则
8. transition period：过渡期
9. regional economic integration：区域性经济一体化
10. non-tariff barriers：非关税壁垒
11. regional trading blocs：区域贸易集团
12. preferential trade agreement：特惠贸易协定
13. access to：有权使用
14. retain：保留
15. eliminate tariffs, quotas and preferences：消除关税；配额以及特惠
16. customs union：关税联盟
17. internal trade：（联盟）内部贸易
18. common external trade policies：共同的对外贸易政策
19. barriers to trade：贸易壁垒
20. fiscal taxes：政府财税
21. the highest remuneration：最高报酬
22. European Community (EC)：欧洲共同市场
23. the European Union (EU)：欧盟
24. economic and monetary union：经济和货币同盟
25. highly unified：高度一体化的

In Practice

➢ **Questions Based on the Text**

I. Decide whether the following statements are true or false according to the text.
1. GATT is a multilateral treaty which was formed in 1947 and had provided the rules for world trade after the WTO came into existence. (　　)
2. China was finally accepted as the 143th member of the WTO on December 11, 2001. (　　)
3. The second stage of economic integration is a customs union. (　　)
4. The lowest level of economic integration is known as complete economic integration.
5. Capital cannot flow to where it can earn the highest remuneration in a common market.

Chapter 1
International Trade Theory and Development

II. Answer these questions according to the text.
1. What is common market?
2. What is the definition of a free trade area? What is it?
3. What do factors of production include?
4. What is the difference between common market and customs union?
5. What is the highest stage of regional economic integration?

III. Translate the following terms.
1. to date _____
2. trade without discrimination _____
3. the multinational trading system _____
4. by reducing tariffs _____
5. in a common market _____
6. enhance regional economic cooperation _____
7. 贸易壁垒 _____
8. 对外贸易 _____
9. 过度期 _____
10. 货币政策 _____
11. 地区发展政策 _____
12. 经济一体化 _____

IV. Fill in the blanks with words or phrases given below. Change the form where necessary.

| discrimination | tariff | transition | integration | retain |

1. We can't _____ against goods from foreign countries.
2. The rights of defendants must be _____.
3. There is a very high _____ on jewelry.
4. This is an _____ of individual countries into trading blocs.
5. There are many students who are in _____ from one programme to another.

| eliminate | transparency | capital | adoption | restriction |

6. The senior partner would provide the initial _____.
7. It is a policy that would _____ inflation.
8. The park is open to the public without _____.
9. There exists the differential _____ of atmosphere.
10. Our country insists the widespread _____ of agricultural technology.

23

| to date | extend into | in addition | be subject to | access to |

11. The members of the board were paid a small allowance _____ their normal salary.
12. These paintings are their finest work _____.
13. No other products shall any longer _____ consolidated industrial and commercial tax.
14. Our expertise _____ all aspects of marketing communication.
15. Our market has complete sets of equipment and easy _____ transportation facilities.

> Workshop

V. Put the following types of regional economic integration into the correct place in the table.

| a. common market   b. free trade area   c. preferential trade agreement |
| d. complete economic integration   e. customs union   f. economic union |

Types	Feature
i	the least level, preferential tariff treatment
ii	the second level, no internal tariff barriers
iii	the third level, a common external tariff
iv	the forth level, factors of production flow internally
v	the fifth level, unified economic policies
vi	the highest level, highly unified economic and social policies

> Case Study

In 1957, six Western European nations—Germany, France, Italy, Belgium, the Netherlands, and Luxembourg—formed the European Economic Community, which has since grown to include most of Europe, now called the European Union (EU), its two biggest effects are on trade policy. First, the members of the European Union have removed all tariffs with respect to each other, thus creating a customs union. Second, the agricultural policy of the European Union has developed into a massive export subsidy program.

The European Union's Common Agricultural Policy (CAP) began not as an export subsidy, but as an effort to guarantee high prices to European farmers by having the European Union buy agricultural products whenever the prices fell below specified support levels.

How does the policy offset the difference between European and world agricultural prices?

Chapter 2

International Trade Policy

1. Tariff Barriers

A tariff, as the term is used in international trade, is a tax on importing a good or service into a country, usually collected by customs officials at the place of entry. Initially, the main aim of tariff is to *raise the government revenue*[1], its protection effect is only regarded to be incidental. Along with the rise of capitalism, policy makers of America and Europe began to use tariff as an effective way to protect their own industries, especially *infant industries*[2].

Although the existence of tariff is not neither rhyme nor reason, it obviously has blocked the development of international trade. After years of continuous effort by GATT and WTO, average tariff rate worldwide has been declining. However, they are still important to most countries. Indeed, only one country in the world, Singapore, has no tariffs at all. In addition, Hong Kong and Macau also have no tariffs as *autonomous customs areas*[3].

Types of Tariffs

If by movement of goods, tariffs can be classified into import duty, export duty and transit duty. Import tariffs have a variety of classifications.

◇ By tax rates

General duty[4]. If a country has no *tariff preference agreement*[5] on certain product with its country of origin, then this product will be taxed at the general duty rate. General duty has the highest rate, and for the most part, is regarded as the basis of tax reduction as per the tariff preference agreement.

MFN duty[6] is a duty for nations entitled to most-favored-nation treatment or trading status. *If a country enters into a tariff treaty that includes the "most-favored-nation" treatment*, *any concession made to one signatory country has to be extended to all participating members*[7]. All members of WTO are entitled to MFN treatment.

Preferential duty[8] is a tariff schedule under which one or more nations are given lower rates or other advantages over others. This means that customs duties for selected imported goods that originate from the signatory countries are lower or totally eliminated.

GSP duty[9] stands for the duty extended under the *General System of Preferences*[10]. The GSP was established in the early 1970s and aimed to give preferential tariff treatment to developing countries until their exporters are in a position to compete in the world market without such preferential treatment. There are 40 donor countries in the world and most of them are developed countries. Among them, only the United States has never selected China as beneficiary country.

◇ By means of collection

A *specific tariff*[11] is stipulated as a money amount per unit of import, such as dollars per ton of coffee beans, or dollars per gearbox. A notable feature of specific tariff is a firm amount only related to the quantity but has nothing to do with quality and price.

An *ad valorem tariff*[12] is a percentage of the estimated market value of the goods when they reach the importing country.

A *compound duty*[13] is a combination of specific tariff and ad valorem tariff. The amount of compound duty is the sum of above mentioned tariffs. For example, America imposes a compound tariff on imports of violins, the duty consists of $1.25 per violin plus 35% of the value, so a consignment of 100 violins valued $10,000 would be imposed total $3,625 compound duty.

Alternative duty[14]. When a particular product is subject to both specific tariff and ad valorem tariff, the customs would impose duties by adopting either of these two tariffs, normally the higher one. An example to help clarify this problem: Country A imposes alternative duty on imports of watches. The specific tariff rate is $10 per watch and the ad valorem tariff rate is 5%, if a wholesaler imports 1,000 watches at the price of $180 per watch, then the duty imposed would be $10,000.

◇ Import surtax[15]

Countervailing duty[16] (CVD), also known as anti-subsidy duty, is import tariff imposed to neutralize the negative effects of subsidies. It is imposed when a foreign country subsidizes its export, injuring domestic producers in the importing country.

Anti-dumping duty[17]. Dumping is the act of charging a lower price for certain goods in a foreign market than their real value in order to promote sales. In this sense, an anti-dumping duty is a temporary duty to imports to offset the effects of dumping.

Emergency duty[18] is imposed when flood of certain products from foreign countries in a short period may harm the manufacturers of domestic similar products. *It is a provisional means to restrain the loss and threats brought by the flood*[19].

Retaliatory duty[20] is a tariff imposed as a means of coercing a foreign government into abandoning discriminatory treatment on trade, investment and intellectual property. *If the unfair treatment is abolished, the imposition of retaliatory tariff will also be terminated*[21].

Basis of Tariffs Collection

A country's tariff schedule is its basis of customs taxation[22]. It is a list of all its import and export duties that consists of three parts: tariff item, description of goods and duty rate. The schedule may have one or more columns. In a single column tariff, the tariff rate is the same for a specific product regardless of the country of origin. A multicolumn schedule discriminates among export countries, with lower rates applying to those with which tariff treaties have been negotiated. The more columns in the tariff schedule, the stronger its flexibility and discrimination present.

Notes

1. raise the government revenue：增加政府的财政收入
2. infant industries：幼稚产业
3. autonomous customs areas：关税自治区
4. general duty：普通关税
5. tariff preference agreement：优惠关税协定
6. MFN duty：最惠国关税
7. If a country enters into a tariff treaty that includes the "most-favored-nation" treatment, any concession made to one signatory country has to be extended to all participating members：如果一个国家加入的关税协定包含最惠国待遇，那么任何给予一方缔约国的特权也要给予所有其他缔约国
8. preferential duty：特惠税
9. GSP duty：普惠制关税
10. General System of Preferences：普遍优惠制

Chapter 2
International Trade Policy

11. specific tariff：从量税
12. ad valorem tariff：从价税
13. compound duty：复合税
14. alternative duty：选择税
15. import surtax：进口附加税
16. countervailing duties：补偿税
17. anti-dumping duty：反倾销税
18. emergency duty：紧急关税
19. It is a provisional means to restrain the loss and threats brought by the flood：这是一种限制由于（产品）大量涌入带来的损失和威胁的临时措施
20. retaliatory duty：报复性关税
21. If the unfair treatment is abolished, the imposition of retaliatory tariff will also be terminated：当不公正待遇被消除，报复性关税的征收也将被终止
22. A country's tariff schedule is its basis of customs taxation：一国的关税税则是其征收关税的依据

In Practice

Questions Based on the Text

I. Decide whether the following statements are true or false according to the text.

1. After years of continuous effort by WTO and GATT, average tariff rate worldwide has been reduced. ( )
2. Tariffs can be classified into import duty, export duty and transit duty according to the tax rates. ( )
3. General duty has the lowest rate. ( )
4. Not all members of WTO are entitled to MFN treatment. ( )
5. A notable feature of specific tariff is a firm amount only related to the quantity but has nothing to do with quality and price. ( )
6. In this sense, an anti-dumping duty is a permanent duty to imports to offset the effects of dumping. ( )
7. Retaliatory tariff is a tariff imposed as a means of coercing a foreign government into abandoning discriminatory treatment on trade. ( )
8. In a single column tariff, the tariff rate is the same for a specific product regardless of the country of origin. ( )

II. Answer these questions according to the text.

1. How many classifications of tariffs are there?
2. What is an anti-dumping duty?
3. What is a notable feature of specific tariff?
4. How many kinds of import surtax? What are they?
5. What is the basis of tariff collection? How does it apply to practice?

> **Business Vocabulary and Useful Expressions**

III. Translate the following terms.

1. average tariff rate _____
2. autonomous customs areas _____
3. preferential duty _____
4. notable feature _____
5. estimate market value _____
6. emergency duty _____
7. 反倾销税 _____
8. 普遍优惠制 _____
9. 从价税 _____
10. 报复性关税 _____
11. 不公正待遇 _____
12. 关税税则 _____

IV. Fill in the blanks with words or phrases given below. Change the form where necessary.

| stipulated | consignment | adopt | clarify | neutralize |

1. They're concerned with the dispatch and receipt of _____.
2. To achieve these ends, we must _____ the above mentioned measures.
3. A delivery date is _____ in the contract.
4. The latest figures should _____ the fears of inflation.
5. A bank spokesman was unable to _____ the situation.

| offset | abandon | discriminatory | abolish | reduction |

6. Protection for domestic industry is admittedly _____.
7. These reforms will _____ racially discriminatory laws.
8. The scheme's investors, fearful of bankruptcy, decided to _____ the project.

9. The increase in pay costs was more than _____ by higher productivity.
10. Many companies have announced dramatic _____ in staff.

| be classified into | as the basis of | entitled to | impose on | regardless of |

11. The fields give high and stable yields _____ climatic circumstances.
12. I am _____ a repayment for the damaged goods.
13. Heavy duties are _____ imports.
14. We all know that culture is _____ the good entrepreneur.
15. Property may _____ real property and personal property.

➢ Workshop

V. Match each term to the correct definition.

| a. emergency duty | b. retaliatory duty |
| c. countervailing duty | d. anti-dumping duty |

(1) A duty imposed to counter the effects of the foreign export subsidy.   (   )
(2) A duty imposed to offset the effects of dumping.   (   )
(3) A duty imposed to reduce the effects of flood of certain product.   (   )
(4) A duty imposed to retaliate the discriminatory treatment.   (   )

➢ Case Study

The EU implements general GSP in ten-year cycles, with the current one adopted in 2004 and set to last from 2006 to 2015. Preferential treatment was given to 179 countries or territories for 7,000 products, among which 3,750 were "sensitive" products that received reductions in tariffs and 3,250 were "non-sensitive" that received duty free access.

In order to benefit from GSP, Least Developed Countries (LDCs) must comply with rules of origin. Rules of origin require goods to originate and be directly transported from the beneficiary country to the EU. If exporters fail to provide proof of origin, they must pay the normal import duties.

What can we learn about the rules of GSP from above passages?

2. Non-Tariff Barriers

With the declining of tariff rates in most industrial countries and developing countries, the use of other barriers to protect domestic industry has increased.

The *non-tariff barrier*[1] (NTB) indicates any policy used to restrict the quantity of imports, other than impose a tariff on imports simply. The wide application of non-tariff barrier is *to avoid violating the rules of GATT*[2] pushing *trade liberalization*[3] initially. As tariff declines and non-tariff rises in importance, GATT begins to take the problems brought by non-tariff barriers seriously. However, less success has been achieved than expected since then. The effect of non-tariff barriers is harder to measure, so it is harder to get agreement on reducing NTBs.

An NTB reduces imports through one or more of the following effects:
- Limiting the quantity of imports directly or indirectly.
- Increasing the cost of imported products.
- Raising the uncertainty of getting import permission.
- Leveling up the risk for importers.

Types of Non-tariff Barriers

Non-tariff barriers have developed several forms, including *import quota*[4], *voluntary export restraint*[5], *technical barriers to trade*[6], and so on.

◇ Import quotas

It is one of the best known NTBs, which means a limit on the total quantity of imports of a product allowed into the country during a certain period of time (for instance, a quarter, half year or a year).

It has two forms:

Absolute quota[7]. The government sets a ceiling for the total quantity or amount permitted into the country of a product, after reaching the ceiling no more of the product is allowed to import. It can be classified into two categories:
- *Global quotas*[8] (unallocated quotas). They are quotas established on the basis of the total quantity or value of imports of specific products, which are filled on a first-come, first-served basis, without reference to countries of origin.
- *Country quotas*[9]. They are quotas of imports reserved for a specific country, which

require the importers to submit certificates of origin. The allocation of quotas depends on the political or economic relations between importing country and exporting country.

Tariff quota[10]. It allows a product imported at a low or zero tariff up to a specified quantity and imposes higher or additional tariff on imports above this quantity. It also can be divided into global quota and country quota in line with countries of origin.

The main difference of these two forms is that absolute quota doesn't *allow excess imports*[11] but tariff quota does.

◇ Voluntary export restraint

The existence of voluntary export restraint (VER) might seem odd. It is a self-restricted policy made by the government of exporting country to limit its export to importing country.

In history, in order to save its *shrinking share*[12] of U. S. auto market and increasing unemployment in auto industry, American government had hinted Japanese government to "voluntarily" restrict its automobiles exports to the United States. For political and economic reasons, Japanese government finally signed an agreement with the U. S. about the voluntary restraint on automobiles export.

◇ Technical Barrier to Trade (TBT)

Technical Barrier to Trade (TBT) is the most popular form of NBT, which involves a serious law and regulations *pertaining to*[13] product standards, including those enforced in the names of health, sanitation, safety and the environment. Standards that accomplish these goals need not discriminate against imports. But, if a government is determined to protect local producers, it can always write rules that can be met by local products than by imported products. For instance, the European Union has banned imports of beef from cattle that have received growth hormones, claiming that it is responding to public concern about health danger.

◇ Other non-tariff barriers

Besides direct measures we have discussed above, there are other barriers that indirectly restrict the imports of foreign products, either by increasing costs or difficulties for importing.

Government procurement[14] means purchases by the government or strongly regulated firms can be directed toward domestically produced goods even when these goods are more expensive than imports. The classic example is the European telecommunications industry. The nations of the European Union in principle have free trade with each other. The main purchasers of telecommunications equipment, are phone companies—and in Europe, these companies have until recently all been *government-owned*[15]. These government-owned telephone companies buy from domestic supplier even when the suppliers charge higher prices than suppliers in other countries. The result is that there is very little trade in telecommunications equipment within Europe.

A *local content requirement*[16] is a regulation that requires some specified fraction of a final good to be produced domestically. In some cases this fraction is specified in physical units, like the U.S. oil import quota in the 1960s. In other cases the requirement is stated in value terms, by requiring that some minimum share of the price of a good represent domestic value added. Local content laws have been widely used by developing countries trying to shift their manufacturing base from assembly back into intermediate goods.

Advance deposit[17] is a policy that requires certain portion of the value of intended imports to be deposited with the government for certain period (usually not a short one), and allows the government to pay low or zero interest on these deposit. The measure will affect the *capital turnover*[18] of importers, thus restricting the scale of import.

Other customs procedures, such as *classification of dutiable product*[19] and *customs valuation of product*[20] will affect the amount of tariff duties owed or the quota limit applied. And, besides that, these procedures can be slow or costly.

Notes

1. non-tariff barrier：非关税壁垒
2. to avoid violating the rules of GATT：为了避免违反关税总协定的规则
3. trade liberalization：贸易自由化
4. import quota：进口配额
5. voluntary export restraint：自动出口限制
6. technical barriers to trade：技术贸易壁垒
7. absolute quota：绝对配额
8. global quotas：全球配额
9. country quotas：国别配额
10. tariff quota：关税配额
11. allow excess imports：允许进口超过配额的部分
12. shrinking share：日渐萎缩的市场份额
13. pertaining to：关于……

Chapter 2
International Trade Policy

14. government procurement：政府采购
15. government-owned：国有
16. local content requirement：本地成分要求
17. advance deposit：进口押金制
18. capital turnover：资金周转
19. classification of dutiable product：征税产品的归类
20. customs valuation of product：海关估价

In Practice

➤ Questions Based on the Text

I. Decide whether the following statements are true or false according to the text.
1. The non-tariff barrier (NTB) indicates any policy used to restrict the quantity of imports, other than impose a tariff on imports simply. ( )
2. As tariff declines and non-tariff rises in importance, GATT begins to take the problems brought by non-tariff barriers seriously. ( )
3. Technical Barrier to Trade (TBT) is the most popular form of NBT. ( )
4. Standards that accomplish these goals need not discriminate against import. ( )
5. The existence of voluntary export restraint (VER) might seem odd. ( )

II. Answer these questions according to the text.
1. What is NTBs?
2. What parts can absolute quota be divided into?
3. What is the main difference between absolute quota and tariff quota?
4. Why is Technical Barrier to Trade (TBT) the most popular form of NBT?
5. If a government is determined to protect local producers, what it can do?

➤ Business Vocabulary and Useful Expressions

III. Translate the following terms.
1. in the name of _____
2. respond to _____
3. auto industry _____
4. import quota _____

35

5. reach the ceiling _____
6. government procurement _____
7. 进口押金制 _____
8. 自动出口限制 _____
9. 进口许可证制 _____
10. 外汇管制 _____
11. 产品规格 _____
12. 垄断力量 _____

IV. Fill in the blanks with words or phrases given below. Change the form where necessary.

| excess | restrict | odd | hint | standard |

1. Edwards has _____ that he will dispose of his majority shareholding.
2. She was charged an _____ of 400 dollars over the amount stated on the bill.
3. The government is considering new laws which will further _____ people's access to firearms.
4. We consider that is the _____ rate of income tax.
5. This student makes a living by doing _____ job.

| involve | enforce | ban | claim | exchange |

6. The union has imposed a _____ on overtime.
7. Not every employee is eligible to _____ unfair dismissal.
8. There have been numerous _____ of views between the two governments.
9. They tried to _____ agreement with their plans.
10. The vast masses there have become _____ in the health campaign.

| pertain to | in the names of | be determined to | respond to | up to |

11. The workers _____ finish the job on time.
12. Jenney's mother made her way _____ bed.
13. How this might _____ choices that people might make is, as yet, unclear.
14. Tom sent a bunch of flower to Jane _____ love.
15. The teacher _____ the question that student put forward.

> Workshop

V. Which of the following are unlikely to be non-tariff barriers?
   a. uses highly-skilled labor

b. preferential duty
c. reduced need for labor
d. low level of automation
e. produces small quantities of products
f. alternative duty
g. countervailing duty
h. produces a simple, uniform product
i. high start-up costs
j. retaliatory duty

➢ Case Study

For much of the 1960s and 1970s, the U.S. auto industry was largely insulated from import competition by the difference in the kinds of cars bought by U.S. and foreign consumers. U.S. buyers, living in a large country with low gasoline taxes, preferred much larger cars than Europeans and Japanese.

In 1979, however, sharp oil price increases and temporary gasoline shortages caused the U.S. market to shift abruptly toward smaller cars. Japanese producers, whose costs had been falling relative to those of their U.S. competitors in any case, moved in to fill the new demand. As the Japanese market share soared and U.S. output fell, strong political forces in the United States demanded protection for the U.S. industry. Rather than act unilaterally and risk creating a trade war, the U.S. government asked the Japanese government to limit its exports. The Japanese, fearing unilateral U.S. protectionist measures if they did not do so, agreed to limit their sales. The first agreement, in 1981, limited Japanese exports to the United States to 1.68 million automobiles. A revision raised to 1.85 million in 1984.

According to the materials, what kind of agreement did Japan and the U.S. reach?

3. Other Trade Policies

Controversy over export behavior and export policy rivals the perennial fights over import barriers[1]. *While governments tend to restrict imports by imposing tariffs or by taking various forms of non-tariff measures, they usually adopt many policies to* promote exports[2]. *However, governments may also* restrict exports[3] *for some particular objectives.*

Export Promotion

◇ Dumping

Dumping is selling exports at a price that is less than normal value or "*fair market value*[4]" (often used in the United States). There are two common definitions of normal value:
- The traditional definition is the price charged in the domestic market. Under this standard, dumping is international price discrimination favoring buyers in foreign markets.
- Another definition is about the cost, saying that the normal price is equal to the possible average total cost of production, including overhead cost and normal profit. Under this definition, dumping is selling products at a price that is even lower than the average cost of the products.

Exporters may engage in dumping for three main reasons:

Seasonal dumping[5] occurs when there is a large stock of certain product left after the selling season, or after its producer has changed to other lines of business. *It is intended to sell off excess inventories of a product in foreign markets*[6].

Predatory dumping[7] occurs when a company temporarily charges a low price in the foreign market, with the purpose of driving its foreign competitors out of business. Once the rivals exit from market, the company can use its monopoly power to raise prices and earn high profits.

Persistent dumping[8] occurs because a company with market power uses price discrimination between domestic and foreign markets *to maximize its total profit*[9]. In general, a company can achieve the purpose if it has more competition in the foreign market and buyers in the home market cannot avoid the high price to get the product.

◇ Export Subsidies

An *export subsidy*[10] is a payment to a firm or an individual that ships a good abroad. An export subsidy can be either direct (cash subsidies granted to exporters) or indirect (preferential treatment to certain exports). When the government offers an export subsidy, shippers will export the good up to the point at which the domestic price exceeds the foreign price by the amount of the subsidy.

◇ Devaluation of home currency

Devaluation means an official lowering of the value of a country's currency[11]. For example, if the Chinese government adjust the exchange rate from USD100 = CNY610 to USD100=CNY620, then Chinese Yuan has been devalued.

Generally, a weaker home currency would result in lower prices of exports and benefit exporters. That is because foreign buyers will pay less for the same product than before, thus *the competitiveness of the product arises*[12]. However, it has to meet two conditions to take effect:
- The extent of devaluation of home currency must exceed that of the appreciation of domestic prices.
- Other countries will not devaluate their own currencies with same extent simultaneously.

◇ Export rebate

Export rebate (exemption), referred to as the export tax rebate[13], its basic meaning is the refund of export products, domestic production and circulation in the actual payment of the product tax, value added tax, business tax and special consumption tax. Export tax rebate system is an important part of *national revenue*[14]. Mainly through the refund of export tax rebate exports to balance domestic taxes already paid the tax burden on domestic products, so that the cost of their products are not included into the international market and foreign products to compete under the same conditions, thereby enhancing competitiveness and expanding exports foreign exchange.

◇ Special economic zone

A *special economic zone*[15] (SEZ) is a geographical region that is designed to export goods and provide employment. SEZ may be exempt from federal laws regarding taxes, quotas, Foreign Direct Investment (FDI)-bans, labor laws and other restrictive laws in order to make the goods manufactured in the SEZ at a globally competitive price.

The category of special economic zone includes:
- Free trade zone. A free trade zone, formerly free port, is an area within which goods may be landed, handled, manufactured or reconfigured, and re-exported without the intervention of the customs authorities. Only when the goods are moved to consumers within the country in which the zone is located do they become subject to the prevailing customs duties. Free-trade zones are organized around major seaports, international airports, and national frontiers—areas with many geographic advantages for trade.

- *Bonded area*[16]. A bonded area, also called bonded warehouse, refers to a secured area in which dutiable goods may be stored, manipulated, or undergo manufacturing operations without payment of duty. It may be managed by the state or by private enterprise. In the latter case a customs bond must be posted with the government.
- *Export processing zone*[17]. An export processing zone can be identified as an industrial estate that are fenced in for producing manufactured goods for export. It is established with special government support including fiscal incentives, tax rebates and other exclusive benefits for the growth of export.

Export Restrictions

Export restrictions are limitations imposed on the quantity of goods exported to certain countries or areas by government in home country. Export restrictions may be applied to following items:

- *Strategic materials, related sophisticated techniques and advanced technical information*[18], for instance, advanced weapons, warships, aircrafts and electronic equipment. These items are restricted for the sake of national security.
- *Scarce resources, including raw materials, intermediate goods and commodities in short supply*[19]. Restraints on said items aim to meet domestic needs for production and consumption.
- *Historical relics and ancient art treasures*[20]. They are so precious cultural heritages that most countries have set strict laws to prevent its outflow.
- Exports under VERs agreement. Violation of VERs may lead to revenge and punishment.
- Product which occupies a dominant position in the world market. To stabilize prices in foreign markets, it is essential to control the quantity of such products exported. For example, OPEC continuously monitors the output and exports of oil of its members.

Notes

1. Controversy over export behavior and export policy rivals the perennial fights over import barriers: 出口及其政策方面的争议可以匹敌针对进口壁垒的长期斗争
2. promote exports: 推动出口
3. restrict exports: 限制进口
4. fair market value: 公平市价

Chapter 2
International Trade Policy

5. seasonal dumping：季节性倾销
6. It is intended to sell off excess inventories of a product in foreign markets：目的是在国外市场把过剩的库存销售出去
7. predatory dumping：掠夺性倾销
8. persistent dumping：持续性倾销
9. to maximize its total profit：使总利润最大化
10. export subsidy：出口补贴
11. devaluation means an official lowering of the value of a country's currency：贬值意味着降低一国货币价值的官方行为
12. the competitiveness of the product arises：产品的竞争力提高了
13. export rebate (exemption), referred to as the export tax rebate：出口退税（免税）指的是出口关税的退还
14. national revenue：国家收入
15. special economic zone：经济特区
16. bonded area：保税区
17. export processing zone：出口加工区
18. Strategic materials, related sophisticated techniques and advanced technical information：战略物资及其相关的尖端技术和先进技术资料
19. Scarce resources, including raw materials, intermediate goods and commodities in short supply：紧缺物资；包括原材料；半制成品和供应不足的商品
20. historical relics and ancient art treasures：历史文物和古代艺术珍品

In Practice

➢ Questions Based on the Text

I. Decide whether the following statements are true or false according to the text.

1. The governments may also restrict exports for some particular objectives. (　　)
2. Dumping is selling exports at a price that is less than normal value or "fair market value". (　　)
3. Seasonal dumping occurs when there is a large stock of certain product left after the selling season, or after its producer has changed to other lines of business. (　　)
4. Once the rivals exit from market, the company can use its monopoly power to raise prices and earn high profits. (　　)
5. Generally, a weaker home currency would result in lower prices of exports and

benefit exporters.   ( )

6. A special economic zone (SEZ) is a geographical region that is designed to export goods and provides employment.   ( )

II. Answer these questions according to the text.
1. What is dumping? How many classifications of dumping are there?
2. What is export subsidy?
3. What are the conditions required to meet if devaluation of home currency takes effect?
4. What does special economic zone (SEZ) refer to? How many kinds of SEZ are there?
5. For what purpose do countries restrict exports?

➢ Business Vocabulary and Useful Expressions

III. Translate the following terms.
1. restrict exports _____
2. domestic market _____
3. average total cost _____
4. fair market value _____
5. domestic and foreign markets _____
6. export subsidy _____
7. 掠夺性倾销 _____
8. 产品竞争力 _____
9. 出口退税 _____
10. 国民收入 _____
11. 出口加工区 _____
12. 自由贸易区 _____

IV. Fill in the blanks with words or phrases given below. Change the form where necessary.

| controversy | rival | definition | occur | stock |

1. The store has a very low turnover of _____.
2. Opportunities for learning _____ spontaneously every day.
3. The announcement ended a protracted _____.
4. He has no serious _____ for the job.

5. According to a strict _____, the expenses of a self-employed person can be deducted from tax.

| grant | exceed | devalued | simultaneous | refund |

6. The pound was _____ against the US dollar.
7. The policy of _____ development of industry and agriculture.
8. Their production costs have _____ £60,000.
9. He refused to _____ them long-term credits.
10. If you're not delighted with your purchase, we guarantee to _____ your money in full.

| be equal to | engage in | refer to | result in | applied to |

11. He _____ a serious study of the problem.
12. In this way theory can be better _____ practice.
13. Acting before thinking always _____ failure.
14. He _____ the occasion.
15. _____ the dictionary when you don't know how to spell a word.

> Workshop

V. Put each of the words under the correct heading.

| a. crude oil | b. warship | c. cotton | d. garments |
| e. ivories | f. toys | g. bullets | h. chocolate |

general products	products with restrictions on exports

> Case Study

The Chinese Ministry of Finance and the State Administration of Taxation have jointly published the Circular on Adjustment of Export Rebate Rate on Certain Textile Products and Garments, announcing the increase of tax rebates for exports of certain textile and garment from 11 percent to 13 percent as of August 1, 2008.

The increase of export rebate is undoubtedly a timely support for the country's export of textile products and garment which have just gone through a "cold spell" (春寒期). Since 2007, Chinese textile enterprise have suffered a lot from the continuous appreciation of RMB, impact of the US subprime crisis, and price rises of raw materials and labor, and the cut of export rebate has further squeezed the paper-thin profit space, almost the last hope for the textile industry. The current increase of export rebate on textile product is undoubtedly good news for textile enterprises. Under the precondition of the product selling price remaining unchanged, a one percentage point increase in the export rebate is equivalent to adding about 1 percent from export to enterprise profits.

From the above article, do you think export rebate is always good for the development of industry and export? Please give another example about the change of export rebate in China.

Chapter 3

Trade Terms and Pricing

1. International Trade Terms

Trade terms are *standardized terms*[1] used in international trade that define the division between exporters and importers of certain minimum obligations, risks and costs involved in transportation of goods. The most widely accepted trade terms are the incoterms rules or international commercial terms published by the *International Chamber of Commerce (ICC)*[2]. The incoterms rules are accepted by governments, legal authorities and *practitioners*[3] worldwide for the *interpretation*[4] of most commonly used terms in international trade. They are intended to reduce or remove altogether uncertainties arising from different interpretation of the rules in different countries.

Incoterms 2010

International commercial terms, also known as "incoterms", are internationally recognized terms defining the responsibilities of exporters and importers in the arrangement of shipments and the transfer of liability involved at different stages of the transaction. Incoterms are made of *a series of three-letter trade terms*[5] related to common sales practices. Incoterms 2010 is the latest version and *came into force*[6] on Jan. 1, 2011. Compared with incoterms 2000, four terms were eliminated (DAF, DEQ, DES, DDU) and two were added: Delivered at Place (DAP) and Delivered at Terminal (DAT). The modifications affect obligations, risk transfer, and cost sharing for the seller and buyer, resulting in better clarification and application of the 11 incoterms, and *consistent with the way global trade is actually conducted*[7] since the last update in 2000. The 11 incoterms *consist of*[8] two groups and are listed below in order of increasing risk/liability to the exporter. Figure 3-1 illustrates how risks, costs and insurance should be *perceived*[9]. Under the revised terms, buyers and sellers are being urged to contract precisely where delivery is made and what charges are covered. *This should avoid double-billing of terminal handling charges at the port of discharge*[10]. References to "ship's rail" were taken out to clarify that delivery means "on-board" the vessel.

◇ Rules for any mode or modes of transportation

EXW—*Ex Works*[11]: Works mean factory, mill and warehouse, which is seller's *premise*[12]. Seller delivers the goods at disposal of buyer at seller's premises. The seller has no responsibility to load the goods on any collecting vehicles and clear the goods for export. It is the most preferable term for those new-to-export because it represents the minimum liability to the seller.

FCA—*Free Carrier*[13]: Seller delivers the goods to the carrier or another person *nominated*[14] by the buyer at the named place (i.e., works, factory, warehouse, etc.). Seller delivers the goods to the carrier and may be responsible for clearing the goods for export. More realistic than EXW because it includes loading at pick-up, which is commonly expected, and sellers are more concerned about export violations.

CPT—*Carriage Paid to*[15]: Seller delivers goods to the carrier or another person nominated by the seller at an agreed place, shifting risk to the buyer. Seller must pay cost of carriage necessary to bring the goods to *the named place of destination*[16]. Seller needs to clear the goods for export, not import.

CIP—Carriage and Insurance Paid to: Seller delivers goods to the carrier or another person nominated by the seller at an agreed place, shifting risk to the buyer. Seller must pay carriage to the named place of destination and insurance cover against the buyer's risk of loss of or damage to the goods during the carriage. *The seller is required to obtain insurance only on minimum cover*[17]. Seller needs to clear the goods for export, not import.

DAT—*Delivered at Terminal*[18]: *Seller delivers when the goods, once unloaded from the arriving means of transport, are placed at the disposal of the buyer at a named terminal at the named port or place of destination*[19]. Seller bears cost, risk and responsibility until goods are unloaded (delivered) at named terminal including *quay, warehouse, yard, or road, rail or air cargo terminal*[20]. *Demurrage or detention charges*[21] may apply to seller. Seller needs to clear goods for export, not import. DAT replaces DEQ, DES in incoterms 2010.

DAP—*Delivered at Place*[22]: Seller delivers when the goods are placed at the disposal of the buyer on the arriving means of transport ready for unloading at the named place of destination. Seller bears cost, risk and responsibility for goods until they were made available to buyer at named place of destination. Seller needs to clear goods for export, not import. DAP is the substitute for DAF, DDU in incoterms 2010.

DDP—*Delivered Duty Paid*[23]: Seller delivers the goods when the goods are placed at the disposal of the buyer, cleared for import on the arriving means of transport ready for unloading at the named place of destination. Seller bears cost, risk and responsibility for cleared goods at named place of destination at buyer's disposal. Buyer is responsible for unloading. Seller is responsible for import clearance, duties and taxes so buyer is not "importer of record". This term should not be used if the seller is unable directly or indirectly to obtain the import license.

◇ Rules for sea and inland waterway transport

FAS—*Free Alongside Ship*[24]: Seller delivers when the goods are placed alongside the vessel (e.g., on a quay or a barge) nominated by the buyer at the named port of shipment. The risk passes to buyer, including payment of all transportation and insurance costs, once delivered alongside the ship (realistically at named port terminal) by the seller. It is seller's obligation to clear the goods for export.

FOB—*Free on Board*[25]: Seller delivers the goods on board the vessel designated by the buyer at the named port of shipment. The risk of loss and damage to the goods passes to buyer, including payment of all transportation and insurance costs, once delivered on board the vessel by the seller. A step further than FAS.

CFR—*Cost and Freight*[26]: Seller delivers the goods on board the vessel designated by the buyer. The risk passes to buyer when on board the vessel. Seller is responsible for arranging and paying cost and freight to the named destination port. A step further than FOB.

CIF—Cost, Insurance and Freight: Seller delivers the goods on board the vessel. The risk passes to buyer when delivered on board the ship. It is seller's obligation to arrange and pay cost, freight and insurance to destination port. Adds insurance costs to CFR.

Matters Needing Attention

Incoterms are not law and have no *binding force*[27] to both parties in international trade if they are not addressed in the sales contract. In addition, they do not:
- Determine ownership or transfer title to the goods.
- Apply to service contracts.
- Cover the goods before or after delivery.

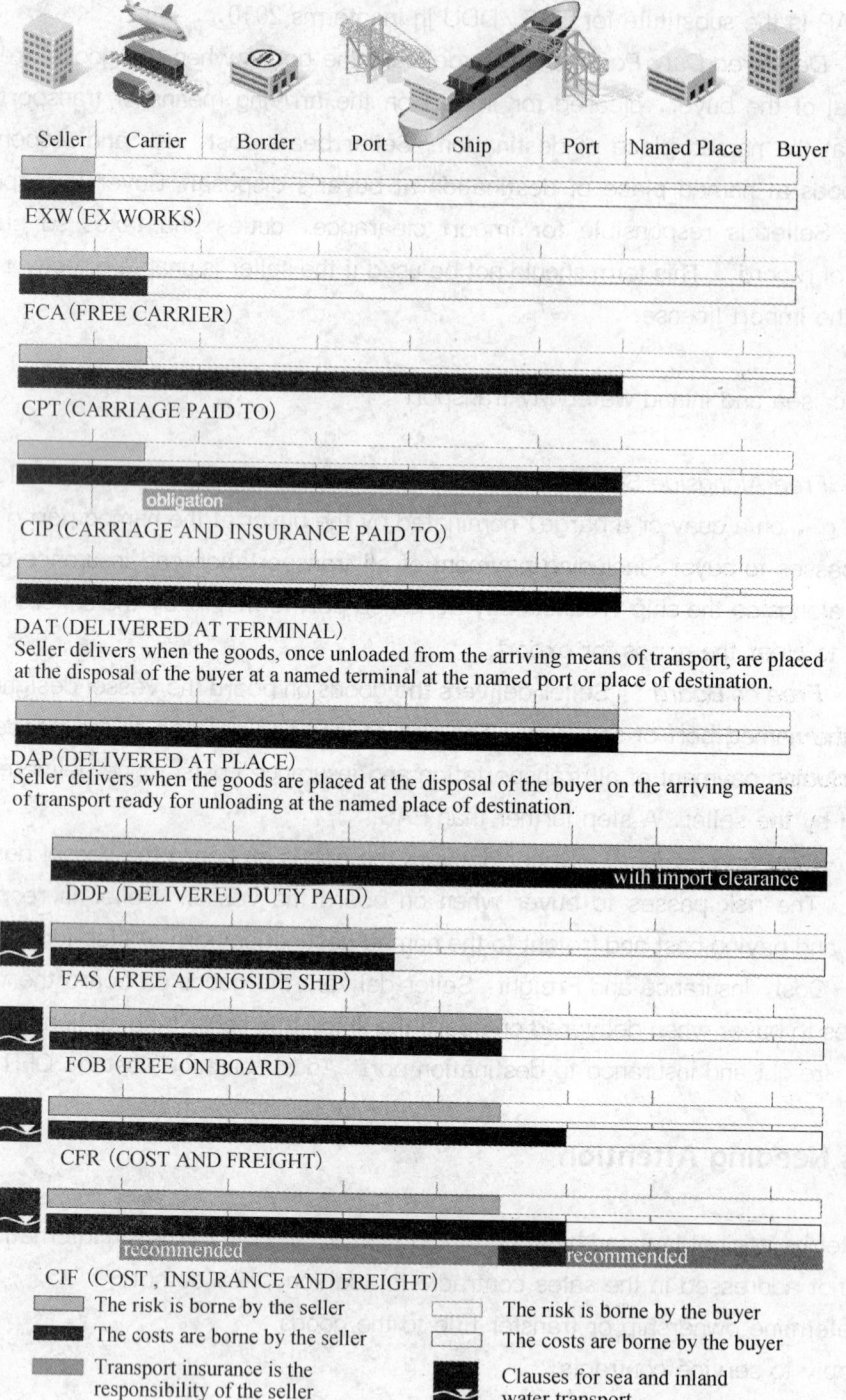

Figure 3-1　Insurance liability, assumption of risks and costs pursuant to Incoterms 2010

Chapter 3
Trade Terms and Pricing

 **Notes**

1. standardized terms：标准化术语
2. International Chamber of Commerce (ICC)：国际商会
3. practitioners：从业者
4. interpretation：解读
5. a series of three-letter trade terms：一系列三个字母的贸易术语
6. came into force：生效
7. consistent with the way global trade is actually conducted：与全球贸易真正的实施方式一致
8. consist of：由……组成
9. perceived：发生
10. This should avoid double-billing of terminal handling charges at the port of discharge：这将避免在重复收取在目的港卸货的费用
11. Ex Works：工厂交货
12. premise：建筑物
13. free carrier：货交承运人
14. nominated：指定的
15. carriage paid to：运费付至
16. the named place of destination：指定目的地
17. The seller is required to obtain insurance only on minimum cover：只要求卖方投保最低限度的保险险别
18. delivered at terminal：终点站交货
19. Seller delivers when the goods, once unloaded from the arriving means of transport, are placed at the disposal of the buyer at a named terminal at the named port or place of destination：卖方在指定的目的港或目的地的指定的终点站卸货后将货物交给买方处置即完成交货
20. quay, warehouse, yard, or road, rail or air cargo terminal：码头；仓库；集装箱堆场或公路,铁路或空运货站
21. demurrage or detention charges：逾期或者滞留费用
22. delivered at place：目的地交货
23. delivered duty paid：完税后交货
24. free alongside ship：船边交货
25. free on board：船上交货
26. cost and freight：成本加运费付至
27. binding force：约束力

In Practice

➢ Questions Based on the Text

I. Decide whether the following statements are true or false according to the text.
1. Incoterms are made of a series of three-letter trade terms. (　)
2. Four terms were eliminated (DAF, DEQ, DES, DDU) and two were added in Incoterms 2000. (　)
3. "Ship's rail" was replaced by "on-board". (　)
4. EXW represents the minimum liability to the buyer. (　)
5. DAP substitutes for DEQ, DES in incoterms 2010. (　)
6. CFR requires seller to bear the cost, freight and insurance. (　)
7. Incoterms are law.

II. Answer these questions according to the text.
1. What do trade terms refer to?
2. What are the incoterms?
3. How many trade terms are there in incoterms 2010?
4. What are the incoterms applied to sea and inland waterway transport?
5. What are the incoterms suitable to any mode of transportation?

➢ Business Vocabulary and Useful Expressions

III. Translate the following terms.
1. trade terms ＿＿＿＿＿＿
2. come into force ＿＿＿＿＿＿
3. consistent with ＿＿＿＿＿＿
4. Ex Works ＿＿＿＿＿＿
5. double-billing ＿＿＿＿＿＿
6. shift risks ＿＿＿＿＿＿
7. 组成 ＿＿＿＿＿＿
8. 指定目的地 ＿＿＿＿＿＿
9. 终点站交货 ＿＿＿＿＿＿
10. 船上交货 ＿＿＿＿＿＿

11. 最低限度 _____
12. 约束力 _____

IV. Fill in the blanks with words or phrases given below. Change the form where necessary.

> interpretation   affect   update   burden   available

1. The season ticket is _____ for three months.
2. This action is open to a number of _____.
3. The tax increases have _____ us all.
4. The economy was further _____ by a flood of refugees.
5. The report gives an _____ on the currency crisis.

> effective   precisely   notify   consolidate   liability

6. Once you contact the card protection scheme your _____ for any loss ends.
7. You need to use legally _____ terms.
8. The company _____ its position in the international market.
9. We'll _____ her to draw up a contract.
10. The agreements will be _____ from November.

> arise from   agree on   be eliminated   consist of   consistent with

11. Our team _____ from the competition in the first round.
12. The atmosphere _____ more than 70% of nitrogen.
13. The country's present difficulties _____ the reduced value of its money.
14. These actions are _____ his principles.
15. They _____ leaving there the next day.

> **Workshop**

V. Put the following trade terms in order of increasing risk/liability to the exporter.

     a. FCA   b. FAS   c. EXW   d. CFR   e. DDP   f. DAT

_____

> **Case Study**

     The buyer and the seller have signed a purchase contract about chemical raw material in accordance with the FOB treaty.

Inspection before shipment, the quality of the goods are in good condition, comply with the provisions of the contract. The goods arrived in the port of destination. After the buyer took delivery of goods, they found that some goods had agglomerated (结块), which meant the original quality had changed. After investigation they confirmed that due to their unsound packing made the goods in transit absorbed moisture in the air that caused such phenomenon. So the buyer filed a claim against the seller. But the seller insisted that their goods were qualified before shipment. The quality change happened during transport.

In accordance with international trade practices, the buyer should take responsibility of the consequences. So they refused to do any compensation accordingly.

How do you think this controversy should be dealt with? Please give your reasons.

2. Pricing

Pricing is one of the key processes in international trade, which determines if the business will be done successfully. How to price properly is closely linked to several factors, such as cost, market condition, quality and competition, etc. In general, an exporter should quote an acceptable price to the customers, and meanwhile, *the price should cover all the costs generated in each transaction*[1].

Elements of Pricing

Pricing involves considering a wide range of particulars like:
- Cost. It includes manufacturing costs, marketing cost, operation cost, and tax, etc. Have a general idea of how much should the *profit margin*[2] be.
- Policies and regulations applied to the target market.
- Competitors' prices of *alternatives*[3] or similar products. Investigate how many competitors there are in the target market, and how about their prices and qualities.
- Market situation. Examine the position of exporters in the target market, if it is a *buyer's market*[4] or a seller's.
- Discount. Use differential strategy for pricing.
- Terms of payment and relevant charges.
- *Currency and fluctuation of foreign exchange rates*[5].
- Other possible factors related to pricing.

Conversion Between Net Prices

Net price[6] refers to a final price without any *commission and discounts*[7]. To indicate the price is net, we usually mark "net" after the terms of trade, for example, EUR 80 per yard CIF London net. According to the incoterms, CFR price could be regarded as *FOB price plus freight charges*[8], and CIF price includes CFR price plus *insurance premium*[9].

◇ *Equations used to convert between FOB price, CFR price and CIF price*:

$$CFR = FOB + freight$$
$$CIF = CFR + insurance\ premium$$
$$= FOB + freight + insurance\ premium$$

◇ *Equations used to convert between FCA price, CPT price and CIP price*:

$$CPT = FCA + freight$$
$$CIP = CPT + insurance\ premium$$
$$= FCA + freight + insurance\ premium$$

Commission and Discount

When pricing, commission or discount sometimes should be involved.

Commission is the remuneration paid to a broker or agent for its service provided to facilitate a transaction[10].

$$Commission = price\ including\ commission \times commission\ rate$$
$$Net\ price = price\ including\ commission - commission$$
$$= price\ including\ commission \times (1 - commission\ rate)$$
$$Price\ including\ commission = \frac{net\ price}{1 - commission\ rate}$$

For example: The original price quoted by the exporter was USD 100 per piece CIF C3% London, later the importer requested to change the quotation to CIF C5%. How will the exporter adjust the price if the net income remains the same as the original one?

The net price = price including commission × (1 − commission rate)
$$= CIF\ C3\% \times (1 - 3\%) = 100 \times 97\% = USD97$$

To remain the same net income, the net price will not be changed, so:

$$The\ new\ price = \frac{net\ price}{1 - commission\ rate} = \frac{97}{1 - 5\%} = USD102.1$$

Discount, or *allowance*[11], is a certain percentage of price reduction and a special favor given by the exporter to the importer. There are different types of discount such as "*quantity discount*[12]"—a discount offered *to induce substantial order*[13], "cash discount"—*an incentive offered for paying an invoice ahead of the scheduled due date*[14], and "special discount" for some special purpose. Discount is specified in the price clause, it is usually expressed as "GBP 80 per metric ton CIF London less 1% discount".

Price Terms in the Contract

The *constitution of price terms*[15] includes two parts: unit price and total amount. Unit price in international trade is more complex than that in domestic trade. It consists of currency, unit amount, unit of measurement and trade terms. For example, JPY 30,000 per unit CFR Yokohama. Total amount is the product of unit price and total quantity.

Ways of price stipulation include:

- *Fixed price*[16]. One of the most common ways of price stipulation is to fix a price that mutually accepted. *The price is irrevocable no matter how the market situation would change during the contract's period of validity*[17]. Fixed price is convenient for settlement but may bring more risks of failure to act the contract.
- *Flexible price*[18]. Due to the uncertainty of market situation, the price may be flexibly defined as "price to be agreed on the date of ×××" or only part of the price is fixed. This kind of pricing is more advantageous in the changing market.
- *Sliding scale price*[19]. If it would take a long period to produce the objective goods of contract, like large machinery and equipment, sliding scale price is suitable for this situation. First, settle a fixed price (or *initial price*[20]) as the basis of price adjustment at the time of contract stipulation, then adjust the final price in line with the changes of salaries and prices of raw materials, etc. For example, company imports a full range of equipment. The initial price is USD 10 million, the percentage of production cost and salaries are "the above initial price will be adjusted according to the following formula based on the wage and price indexes published by ××× (organization) as of ××× (month), 20××.

Notes

1. The price should cover all the costs generated in each transaction: 价格必须涵盖单笔交易所产生的一切费用

Chapter 3
Trade Terms and Pricing

2. profit margin：利润率
3. alternatives：替代品
4. buyer's market：买方市场
5. currency and fluctuation of foreign exchange rates：货币及汇率的变动
6. net price：净价
7. commission and discounts：佣金和折扣
8. FOB price plus freight charges：FOB 价加上运费
9. insurance premium：保费
10. Commission is the remuneration paid to a broker or agent for its service provided to facilitate a transaction：佣金是支付给中介或代理为促成交易提供服务的报酬
11. allowance：折扣
12. quantity discount：大量购买折扣
13. to induce substantial order：吸引大笔订单
14. an incentive offered for paying an invoice ahead of the scheduled due date：激励对方在指定日期之前付清货款的奖励
15. constitution of price terms：价格条款的组成
16. fixed price：固定价格
17. The price is irrevocable no matter how the market situation would change during the contract's period of validity：无论在合同的有效期间市场行情如何变动，价格都是不可更改的
18. flexible price：可变价格
19. sliding scale price：滑动价格
20. initial price：初始价格

In Practice

➢ Questions Based on the Text

I. Decide whether the following statements are true or false according to the text.

1. How to price properly is closely linked to several factors, such as cost, market condition, quality and competition, etc.　　　　　　　　　　　　　　　(　)
2. Due to the uncertainty of market situation, the price may be flexibly defined as "price to be agreed on the date of ×××".　　　　　　　　　　　　(　)
3. Commission is the remuneration paid to a broker or agent for its service provided to facilitate a transaction.　　　　　　　　　　　　　　　　　　　　(　)

55

4. The constitution of price terms includes three parts: unit price and total amount etc.
   (   )

5. If it would take a long period to produce the objective goods of contract, like large machinery and equipment, sliding scale price is suitable for this situation. (   )

II. Answer these questions according to the text.
   1. Why do we say pricing is one of the key processes in international trade?
   2. What factors should be taken into consideration when pricing?
   3. What does net price refer to?
   4. What is commission?
   5. How many ways are there to price a product? What are they?

➤ Business Vocabulary and Useful Expressions

III. Translate the following terms.
   1. profit margin _____
   2. target market _____
   3. relevant charges _____
   4. foreign exchange rates _____
   5. net price _____
   6. FOB price _____
   7. 保费 _____
   8. 买方市场 _____
   9. 大量购买折扣 _____
   10. 大笔订单 _____
   11. 初始价格 _____
   12. 单价 _____

IV. Fill in the blanks with words or phrases given below. Change the form where necessary.

   convert   insurance   provided   discount   incentive

   1. The other banks are going to be very eager to help, _____ that they see that he has a specific plan.
   2. Full-time staff get a 20 per cent _____.
   3. The signal will be _____ to/into digital code.
   4. Many companies in Britain are keen on the idea of tax _____ for R & D.

56

5. The _____ will cover all the loss in this case.

| complex | stipulation | mutually | adjustment | initial |

6. The business quickly repaid the _____ outlay on advertising.
7. The East and the West can work together for their _____ benefit and progress.
8. He put over a _____ and difficult business deal.
9. The only _____ the building society makes is that house must be insured.
10. Compensation could be made by _____ to taxation.

| be involved in | consist of | be convenient for | due to | a full range of |

11. The entire world _____ matter.
12. We cut down the number of people who needed to _____ important decisions.
13. The insurance company will refund any amount _____ you.
14. When would it _____ you to go?
15. We have _____ products from cosmetics to skin cleansers and moisturizers.

➤ Workshop

V. Make quotations according to the following particulars.

1. _____ Unit price is USD 25, 8000 yards, ship to New York, FOB.
2. _____ Unit price is EUR 50, 6000 units, ship to Antwerp, CIF.
3. _____ Unit price is JPY 30000, 500 sets, ship to Yokohama, FOB.
4. _____ Unit price is AUD 75, 2000 dozens, ship to Melbourne, CFR.
5. _____ Unit price is CAD 15, with commission 5%, 12,000 bottles, ship to Vancouver, CIF.

➤ Case Study

Value pricing can mean many things to marketers. To some, it means price cutting. To others, it means special deals, such as providing more of a product at the same price. Still to others, it means a new image—one that convinces consumers they're receiving a good deal. No matter how it's defined, however, value pricing has become a prime strategy for wooing consumers.

In a recent world tour, General Electric Chairman Jack Welch noted that customers around the global are now more interested in price than technology. "The value decade is upon us," he stated. "If you can't sell a top-quality product at the world's lowest price, you're going to be out of the game." As a result, in products ranging from refrigerators to CAT scanners and jet engines, GE is working to offer basic, dependable units at unbeatable prices.

Value pricing involves more than just cutting prices. It means finding the delicate balance between quality and price that gives target consumers the value they seek. To consumers, "Value is not the same as cheap." Value pricing requires price cutting coupled with findings ways to maintain or even improve quality while still making a profit.

Try to think over what the statement "value pricing involve more than just cutting prices" means?

Chapter 4

International Trade Procedure

In fact, the basic procedures of international trade may be *summed up*[1] in the following three stages, namely, *launching a profitable transaction negotiation of terms and conditions for the formation of a contract, and performance of a contract*[2]. In this chapter, we will focus on the three stages.

1. Launching a Profitable Transaction

When you make the decision to start an international trade business, you have to make a market research to collect some related information about the international market so as to *study and predict the future movement*[3] of your business. The market survey usually devotes to the related product you may choose, *the target market conditions*[4] and *the potential business partners*[5].

Selecting a Suitable Product

If your firm already manufactures merchandise or provides a service, that product or service is what you sell. But, for your own import/export business, your job will be to sell someone else's product or service. In other words, you will be the *middleman*[6] and choose a product you prefer.

There are many areas you can pick like *agriculture, textiles, apparel & sporting goods, used and reconditioned equipment, health technology, marine technology, consumer goods & home furnishings, and publishing*[7]. Businessmen usually begin with a single product or service they know and understand, or have experience with. Product selection is a personal decision, but the decision should *make common sense*[8].

For example, if you are an engineer, don't start with fashionable textiles or health technology. Or, if you are a doctor, don't begin by exporting *gas turbine engines*[9] because you don't know this area at all before you begin. After all, start your business with a product or service with which you have an advantage because of prior knowledge.

Selecting a Target Market

Once you have decided which type of product or service you want to do, *an in-depth market research*[10] should be done to find out things like your products potential in a given market, the market's business practices and your best prospects for success. To select a target market, you will have to consider its political and economic conditions, its foreign policy and trade policy, its usual exporting and importing commodities and the information on trade barriers and restrictions, etc.

Besides, before determining your target customer groups in the target market, you will have to make a survey to gain the information as the following:

◇ The size of the market

Verify the size of the market by conducting customer surveys to determine whether your product or service *fits an unmet need*[11] in the target market. Find out whether there has been any resistance to other companies entering the market and why.

◇ The related product

Aim at[12] the details of the related products, especially the varieties, styles, qualities, packing, etc.

◇ Target customers

Evaluate which *customer segments*[13] have the financial resources to purchase your product or service and are most likely your target customers.

◇ The pricing structure

Determine the pricing structure for your products, which is made on the basis of the market survey. It directly affects the profit of the exporter. *What are taken into consideration when setting a price are the demand of the target market, the advantages and disadvantages of the exporting products, and cost accounting, etc*[14]. It will give you the best chance of generating sales while still maintaining profitability.

Selecting a Potential Partner

Selecting a potential business partner is vital to the success of any exporter or any importer. Importers and exporters *need contacts to get started*[15].

The exporter must sure that his or her foreign partner has the ability to buy the product or service provided. The importer, on the other hand, must find an overseas manufacturer or middleman who intends to sell the product or service.

Many countries have various trade associations in which foreign investors can meet local business people. The product or service you select will *fall into a certain industry classification*[16] and that industry very likely has an association. Begin looking for manufacturers of your product or service in the appropriate association or publication. Next, contact the nearest *consulate office*, *foreign country's International Chamber of Commerce*, *foreign exchange banks or trade directors*[17].

Attending trade fairs or shows is an excellent way to make business contacts and research foreign markets. At these shows, importers and exporters can make contacts and learn more about products, markets, potential customers and distributors. In addition, there are other sources available for international traders to find the potential business partners: direct sales, direct mail, manufacturer's representatives, as well as wholesalers.

When you find out the contact, the next step is to have a communication and *get acquainted with*[18] the company you are thinking about having as a business partner. This can be done through emails, repeated phone conversations or letters to ask for further information.

Of course, sometimes taking a trip to the country with which you intend to trade is necessary. It will *make a big difference*[19] since face-to-face communications, in-person meetings, business luncheons, and general business meetings will help you know more about your potential business partner and make sure whether it is the right one that fits for your needs and wants.

Never start the business with your potential business partner before identifying the following information: *credit reference*[20], financial status, business range, business mode, *annual sales volume*[21].

Furthermore, but not the least, in some business, the exporter may be required to *apply for an exporting license or a quota*[22] according to the regulations of the country. That means you have to make sure whether the product you intend to export is within some certain export controls. It is the exporter's duty to obtain the exporting license or the quota before the negotiation of trade terms and conditions. It is also applicable to the importer. Actually, countries have more import controls than export controls on commodities in international trade. The importer also must make sure whether a license is needed and can be obtained before the transaction is started.

Notes

1. summed up：总结
2. launching a profitable transaction, negotiation of terms and conditions for the formation of a contract and performance of a contract：推出可盈利交易，为形成合同洽谈条款以及履行
3. study and predict the future movement of your business：研究并预测你的企业的将来动态
4. the target market conditions：目标市场的状况
5. the potential business partners：潜在的合作伙伴
6. middleman：中间人
7. agriculture, textiles, apparel & sporting goods, used and reconditioned equipment, health technology, marine technology, consumer goods & home furnishings, and publishing：农产品、纺织品、服装、体育用品、二手翻新设备、医疗技术、航海技术、日用品、家庭陈设及出版业
8. make common sense：符合常理
9. gas turbine engines：燃气涡轮发动机
10. an in-depth market research：深入的市场调查
11. fit an unmet need：填补一个未满足的需求
12. aim at：针对，以……为目标
13. customer segments：客户群
14. What are taken into consideration when setting a price are the demand of the target market, the advantages and disadvantages of the exporting products, and cost accounting, etc.：在制定价格时,需要考虑的是目标市场的需求、出口产品的优缺点和成本核算等
15. need contact to get started：需要贸易对象来开展业务
16. fall into a certain industry classification：属于某个产业门类
17. consulate office, foreign country's International Chamber of Commerce, foreign exchange banks or trade directors：领事馆、外国的国际商会、外汇银行或贸易指南
18. get acquainted with：知晓；了解
19. make a big difference：（其结果）大不一样
20. credit reference：信用证明

21. annual sales volume：年销售额
22. apply for an exporting license or a quota：申请出口许可证或配额

In Practice

➤ Questions Based on the Text

I. Decide whether the following statements are true or false according to the text.

1. The market survey is a way to collect some related information about the international market, which helps to make correct decisions. (　　)
2. A middleman is a person or company that buys things from the people who produce them and sells them to the people who want to buy them. (　　)
3. If you are a fashion designer, you can't begin your business with fashionable textiles. (　　)
4. When making price, you should consider cost accounting that is only element. (　　)
5. Factors related to the potential partner, its credit reference and business range may well worth investigating. (　　)
6. A certain association in some countries is the one where foreign traders can meet local businesspeople. (　　)
7. Face-to-face communication is the only way to help you know the potential partner. (　　)
8. In international trade, most countries have more export controls than import controls on commodities. (　　)

II. Answer these questions according to the text.

1. What does the market survey focus on?
2. Why do businessmen often start their business with a product they know?
3. What do you consider when selecting a target market?
4. How channels are there when you seek the potential partner? What are they?
5. Why should exporters apply for a license? What about importers?

➤ Business Vocabulary and Useful Expressions

III. Translate the following terms.

1. terms and conditions

2. devotes to _____
3. potential business partners _____
4. customer segments _____
5. make a big difference _____
6. annual sales volume _____
7. 目标市场 _____
8. 深入的市场调查 _____
9. 信用证明 _____
10. 申请出口许可证 _____
11. 国际商会 _____
12. 推出盈利交易 _____

IV. Fill in the blanks with words or phrases given below. Change the form where necessary.

| launch   fulfillment   recondition   prior   restriction |

1. A heavily damaged machine can't be _____.
2. The musical theater company is about to _____ a new performer on the musical world.
3. I have a _____ engagement and so can't go with you.
4. They exported commodities there without _____.
5. The _____ of work safety control indicators was relatively good.

| survey   variety   consulate   profitability   quota |

6. These costs will impact on our _____.
7. The United States _____ can provide further information about these requirements.
8. The library routinely handles a wide _____ of enquiries.
9. A _____ of 100 winter-swimmers in different age groups indicates that 70% originally suffered from diseases.
10. The _____ of immigrants for this year has already been filled.

| aim at   take into consideration   convince... of   make a difference   annual sales volume |

11. Both past and future assessment of accounts must be _____.
12. Your support will certainly _____ in our cause.
13. The _____ of our market reaches RMB 5 trillion which indicates a bright

future.
14. Businesses will have to _____ long-term growth.
15. We were able to _____ the students _____ the need for wider reading.

> **Workshop**

V. **Match each term to the correct definition.**

| a. Abusiness partner | b. Acredit reference | c. A target market | d. A Trade barrier |
| e. An import quota | f. A trade fair | g. An association | |

(1) It is a government-induced restriction on international trade. It can take many forms, including tariff and non-tariff. ( )

(2) It is an individual or company who has some degree of involvement with another entity's business dealings. The term is also frequently used for two businesses that cooperate, to any degree, such as a computer manufacturer who works exclusively with another company who supplies them with parts. ( )

(3) It is a group of customers towards which a business has decided to aim its marketing efforts and ultimately its merchandise. ( )

(4) It is information, the name of an individual, or the name of an organization that can provide details about an individual's past track record with credit. ( )

(5) It may also refer to a corporate body consisting of a group of associated persons who usually meet periodically because of common profession, objectives, or interests. ( )

(6) It is an exhibition organized so that companies in a specific industry can showcase and demonstrate their latest products, service, study activities of rivals and examine recent market trends and opportunities. ( )

(7) It is a limit on the quantity of a product that can be produced abroad and sold domestically. ( )

> **Case Study**

A Chinese exchange student, Lu lin, is pursuing his master degree in Massachusetts Institute of Technology. He is interested in playing golf and knows that the sport is growing in China. Then he intends to start a business exporting American golf sporting goods to his home country. He knows a golf club very well, in which he was a number before. So it is not very difficult for him to negotiate with the manager of this golf club and he is quickly in business.

However, obviously, the market is developing more slowly than he expected after the first dealing.

If you were Lu Jin, how will you develop your market? What channels can he contact with?

2. Business Negotiation and Trade Contract

Business negotiation[1] is a bargaining situation in which the exporter and the importer have a *common interest*[2] to cooperate, but at the same time have conflicting interests over exactly how to share. It is an important part of conducting a foreign trade for both parties to *reach an agreement*[3] on relevant terms and conditions, such as price, payment, quality and delivery etc.

In most cases, business negotiation of international trade is done by email which is the most efficient, by telex or by fax. Sometimes, negotiations through telephone or face-to-face communication are usual means the traders use. It often *commences with*[4] an enquiry or *Request For Quote*[5] (*RFQ*) sent by the importer to the exporter.

Enquiry

An enquiry is a request for the detailed information about what the buyer intends to purchase, *especially the availability or supply of goods, catalogues, prices, discounts, delivery, terms of payment*[6], etc. A Request For Quote is a variation of a Request For Proposal (RFP), and typically provides more information to the bidder about the project's requirements. It often requires the bidder to *break down costs*[7] for each phase of the project so as to allow the *soliciting company*[8] to compare different bids.

Enquiries or RFQs vary with their different contents, different purposes and different backgrounds. However, each one should be brief, specific, courteous and reasonable. The following are the two examples of an enquiry and a RFQ:

◇ An enquiry

> We are interested in your Chinese Walnut in shell 2010 crop. Would you be kind enough to quote the price CIF London, stating your earliest delivery time, terms of payment and discounts for *regular purchases*[9]?

Chapter 4
International Trade Procedure

◇ A RFQ

> Please *quote your best price and delivery*[10] on the attached RFQ #3706E by 2/17/2014. Please return your quote on our attached form and please fill in your company name and contact information where highlighted when you reply.

Any enquiry means potential business. It is of great importance for the seller to reply without any delay and *make an offer*[11] promptly and carefully.

Offer

An offer is a proposal to supply goods on the terms and conditions stated, which is the reply made by a seller to the enquiry. An offer may either be *a firm offer*[12] within a stated time or be *a non-firm offer*[13] without a certain time limit.

◇ A firm offer

In a firm offer, a seller not only quotes the price of the goods he wants to sell but also indicates all necessary terms of sales, such as delivery, shipping and terms of payment as well as names of goods, quality, specifications, quantity, packing and insurance.

The most important requirement in a firm offer is to state the *validity period*[14]. It is a *contractual obligation*[15], once it is properly accepted by the offeree within the validity of the offer, this firm offer cannot be withdrawn and it will *have a binding force*[16] upon both the offeror and offeree. A firm offer is also called "offer with engagement". Here is an example of a firm offer.

> In reply, we would like to make you, subject to your reply reaching us by the end of this month, the following offer:
>
> | Name of Commodity | Quantity | Unit Price (CIF London) | Total Price |
> | --- | --- | --- | --- |
> | Coffer Maker (Model A) | 100 sets | US $360 | US $36,000 |
> | Coffer Maker (Model B) | 60 sets | US $405 | US $24,300 |
>
> Packing: Standard Export Packing.
> Shipment: In one week after sample approval.
> Payment: 1/2 by T/T before shipment and 1/2 by T/T after receipt of the goods.

◇ A non-firm offer

Contrary to a firm offer, an offer without engagement is a non-firm offer often made by sending pricelists and catalogues, stating terms of payment, shipping and packing without the validity period. It is not final, and often uses such words as "*subject to our final confirmation*[17]". Therefore, a non-firm offer does not have any binding force. The following for example, is a non-firm offer of this kind.

> We thank you and confirm the receipt of your letter of February 15th. We are now making you the following offer subject to our final confirmation:
>
> We can offer 5,000 pcs at US $50 per one on CIF C3% basis. The shipment is to be made within 35 days after the order confirmed. *We require payment by confirmed, irrevocable letter of credit at sight in our favor*[18].

Counter-offer

When an offeree partly agrees or totally disagrees with the offer, the offeree will make a counter-offer to put forward some additions, modification, limitations, etc. as to the basic terms and conditions contained in the offer.

A counter-offer, in fact, is a rejection of the offer. So, it is also called a new offer at the same time, the original offer lapses. In a counter-offer a new price or other new terms are suggested. A letter of counter-offer, for example, is as follows.

> Thanks for your offer of June 20th and we found that the price for Coffee Makers (Model A) seems reasonable. However, the price for Model B is on the high side, and much higher than that of the other competitor. It is currently possible for us to purchase at your quoted price for Model B in the Toronto market.
>
> Please do your best to make the cost down in every respect. We will place the order with you if you could accept our price of USD $380 per one for Model B.

Acceptance

An acceptance or a confirmation is an unreserved assent of the buyers or the sellers, who after mutual negotiations are willing to enter into a contract in accordance with terms and conditions agreed upon[19]. It is a statement made by oral or written or other conduct of the offeree, the particular person or a group of persons, who are clearly stipulated in a firm offer indicating assent to an offer.

In light of[20] the usual practice in foreign trade, an acceptance should abide by[21] the following requirements:
- It must be *absolute and unconditional*[22].
- It can be made by an offeree's act.
- It must be clearly expressed by an offeree's verbal or written statement.
- It must be made by offeree within the valid period of a firm offer.

Conclusion of a Contract

Once an acceptance is effectively made, the contract is concluded. *A contract is an arrangement that creates an obligation, which is a binding, legally enforceable agreement between two or more competent parties*[23].

A contract drafted by the seller is called a *sales contract*[24]/confirmation, while that worked out by the buyer is called a *purchase contract*[25]/confirmation. Legally, both the sales contract and the sales confirmation are equally binding on the parties. On the whole, the former is more formal, and the latter, less formal.

A contract proper includes: the full names of the buyer and the seller; the commodities involved; all the terms and conditions agreed upon; indication of the number of original copies of the contract, the term of validity and possible extension of the contract. Here is a sample of a contract:

```
                          CONTRACT
                                    NO:
                                    DATE:

THE BUYER: THALE INC              THE SELLER: SHANGHAI BEITE CO., LTD
           201 WSET CREEK BLVD                588 YELUO RD.
           BRAMPTON ON L6T 5S6                200050 SHANGHAI
           CANADA                             CHINA
```

This Contract is made by and between the Buyers and the Sellers, in November 21, 2013 whereby the Buyers agree to buy and the Sellers agree to sell the under mentioned commodity according to the terms and conditions stipulated below:

（continued）

Name of Commodity	Quantity	Unit Price（CIF London）	Total Price
Coffer Maker（Model A）	100 sets	US $360	US $36,000

PACKING：Standard Export Packing.
SHIPMENT：In one week after sample approval.
SHIPPING MARK：The Seller shall mark on each package with fadeless paint the package number, gross weight, measurements.
INSURANCE：To be covered by the Buyer.
PAYMENT：1/2 by T/T before shipment and 1/2 by T/T after receipt of the goods.
PORT OF SHIPMENT：Shanghai, China
PORT OF DESTINATION：Toronto, Canada
REMARK：Please sign and return one Original of the Sales Contract to us for file.

  THE BUYER   THE SELLER

 Notes

1. business negotiation：商务谈判
2. common interest：共同利益
3. reach an agreement：达成一致意见
4. commences with：从……开始
5. Request For Quote(RFQ)：询价
6. especially the availability or supply of goods, catalogues, prices, discounts, delivery, terms of payment：特别是可提供的货物、目录、价格、折扣、交货期及付款方式
7. break down costs：将成本进行分项报价
8. soliciting company：询价的公司
9. regular purchases：常规采购
10. quote your best price and delivery：报出你们最低的价格和交货期
11. make an offer：报盘
12. a firm offer：实盘
13. a non-firm offer：虚盘

14. validity period：有效期
15. contractual obligation：合同义务；契约债务
16. have a binding force：有约束力
17. subject to our final confirmation：以我方最后确认为准
18. We require payment by confirmed, irrevocable letter of credit at sight in our favor：我们要求的付款方式是以我方为受益人的，保兑的、不可撤销的即期信用证
19. An acceptance or a confirmation is an unreserved assent of the buyers or the sellers, who after mutual negotiations are willing to enter into a contract in accordance with terms and conditions agreed upon：一份接受或确认是指买卖双方在互惠互利的商务洽谈后，愿意根据双方达成一致的条件条款来签订合同，并无条件地同意各项交易条件的一种表示
20. in light of：按照；根据
21. abide by：遵守
22. absolute and unconditional：绝对的和无条件的
23. A contract is an arrangement that creates an obligation, which is a binding, legally enforceable agreement between two or more competent parties：合同是指两方或更多责任方之间签订的一份绑定双方责任义务，法律上强制执行的协议
24. sales contract：销售合同
25. purchase contract：采购合同

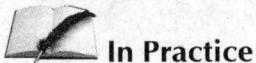 In Practice

> Questions Based on the Text

I. Decide whether the following statements are true or false according to the text.

1. All of the interests, which the importer and the exporter have, definitely conflict. ( )

2. An enquiry is a request for business information, such as price lists, catalogue, samples, and details about the goods or trade terms. ( )

3. On receiving the enquiry, it is a regular practice that the exporter should reply to it without delay. ( )

4. There are two kinds of offers, one is the firm offer, the other, non-firm offer. ( )

5. If the offer has a restrictive condition, i.e., "subject to our final confirmation", then it's a firm offer regarded as an invitation for offer. ( )

6. If offeree accepts the original offer after he made a counter-offer, the contract is invalid. ( )
7. An acceptance can be made by offeree after the valid period of a firm offer. ( )
8. A contract can be worked out either by the seller or the buyer, and is called a sales contract or a purchase contract respectively. ( )

II. Answer these questions according to the text.
1. What is an enquiry?
2. What is the key point of a firm offer?
3. When is a counter-offer made in a business negotiation?
4. What requirements should an acceptance abide by?
5. What does a contract contain?

➤ Business Vocabulary and Useful Expressions

III. Translate the following terms.
1. commences with _____
2. in light of _____
3. common interest _____
4. purchase contract _____
5. have a binding force _____
6. confirmed, irrevocable letter of credit at sight _____
7. 常规采购 _____
8. 报盘 _____
9. 以我方最后确认为准 _____
10. 将成本进行分项报价 _____
11. 达成一致意见 _____
12. 以我方为受益人 _____

IV. Fill in the blanks with words or phrases given below. Change the form where necessary.

| bargaining | common | availability | courteous | proposal |

1. When _____, both of you should know what price is fair.
2. Before travelling we must ensure the _____ of petrol and oil.
3. She needed to soften her request to make it as polite and _____ as she could.
4. We just pay the price of something directly without _____.

5. It is _____ knowledge that the earth is round.

| obligation withdraw engagement assent competent |

6. If you want to learn English, you must first find a _____ teacher.
7. The end of this discussion was another _____ at twenty per week.
8. All foreign troops must be _____ immediately and unconditionally.
9. She is under an _____ to her adoptive father.
10. The government gave its _____ to the new project.

| commence with abide by break down quote one's price in one's favor |

11. Negotiations between the seller and the buyer have _____.
12. This chapter _____ an analysis of individual buying behavior.
13. They should continue to _____ what has been agreed on.
14. If you _____ and delivery before this weekend, we will consider placing the order with you.
15. We'd like you to establish a local letter of credit _____.

➢ Workshop

V. Judge which one of the following intends to make.

a. an enquiry	b. an invitation to make an offer
c. an offer (firm or non-firm)	d. a counter-offer
e. an acceptance	

1. We are in the market for Chinese green tea. Would you please to make your best possible firm offer on CIF New York, stating terms of payment and the earliest date of shipment?   (   )
2. Thanks for your quotation, say, USD $76 per one for these machining parts. But it is higher than our target price. If the price can go down 5%, we are happy to fix the order.   (   )
3. We are glad to inform you that we have accepted your offer dated July 1st, 2013. Please let us have your earliest reply by email.   (   )
4. We offer subject to your reply here by 10th May our time, 100 M/T beans at USD $280 on FOB basis, July shipment, payment by sight L/C.   (   )
5. Your quotation of box fans is rather high. Our client will only agree to accept if it is changed from FOB Shanghai to CIF San Francisco.   (   )

6. We are making you, subject to our final confirmation, the following offer: 50 metric tons of Walnut meat, F.A.Q. 2012 Crop, at USD $260 per metric ton CIF Odense. ( )
7. Your website interests us. Please send your EX-work price for your new washing machines. ( )

➢ Case Study

On Dec. 21st, Company A from Britain offered to sell goods to Company B from Germany, at the unit price of USD 380 CIF London, "Offer valid if reply here Dec. 26th". On Dec. 23rd Company B emailed back. "Offer accepted if USD 350 per one". As Company A is considering the bid, the market price went over USD 380. On Dec. 25th, Company B emailed an unconditional acceptance of Company A's initial offer.

Could Company A reject Company B's acceptance?

3. Performance of the Contract

In international trade, once a contract is concluded, both the seller and the buyer should *perform their rights and obligation*[1]. The seller must deliver the goods, hand over any documents relating to them and *transfer the property in the goods*[2] while the buyer must pay the price for the goods and *take delivery of*[3] them as required by the contract.

The specific procedures of performance of the contract may be different since the terms and conditions included in each contract vary. *Although within some countries, commercial credit such as open account, remittance, D/A is commonly used for the payment and settlement, L/C is still asked for payment by Chinese traders due to its safety*[4].

Therefore, this chapter will briefly introduce the procedures both the exporter and the importer need to go through particularly *under L/C payment terms*[5].

Export Procedures

China is one of the biggest export countries in the world. It mainly exports electrical machinery, apparel, textiles, iron, steel and medical equipment under CIF terms and by payment of L/C. Therefore, a lot of work is involved in implementing this kind of contracts: *cargo readiness*[6], letter of credit, *customs clearance*[7], shipment and document and payment. The following is a brief account of the possible steps in an export transaction.

◇ Cargo readiness

Immediately after the contract is signed, the exporter should start to ensure the goods are to be made ready for shipment before the *stipulated delivery time*[8]. The quantity, quality, packaging and marking of the goods must strictly follow the stipulation in the sales contract. If the goods need to be inspected before shipment, the inspection should be conducted in time and necessary inspection certificates must be made available. If any certificate is required in the contract, the exporter has to get them ready as stipulated.

◇ Letter of credit

If the payment is to be made by letter of credit, the exporter should require the importer to establish the L/C on time. However, sometimes it may be delayed for many unexpected reasons. To *smooth the transaction*[9], the exporter should urge the importer to *expedite the opening of L/C*[10]. The exporter may wait until the L/C is opened to arrange the cargo readiness.

It is necessary for the exporter to check the L/C against the sales contract when receiving the L/C. Only when all the terms in the L/C are *consistent with*[11] the terms of the sales contract can the exporter *proceed to*[12] the shipment of the goods. If any discrepancies are found, the exporter should ask the importer to amend the L/C as soon as possible to avoid further trouble.

◇ Customs clearance

The Customers Law of the People's Republic of China prescribes that the clearance of export goods shall be made by the consignor 24 hours *prior to*[13] loading. Therefore, before shipping the exporter should declare the export goods to the customs by filling in certain customs and submitting appropriate documents such as *commercial invoice*, *export license*, *copy of sales contract and inspection certificates*[14], etc. The customs will inspect the export goods and decide if the shipment can be cleared through customs. Once the goods are cleared, shipment can be made anytime.

◇ Shipment

Whatever being in FOB or CIF, the exporter needs to connect with shipment agency to *book the shipping space*[15] two weeks before delivery. Receiving a confirmation of shipping from the carrier, the exporter may start to prepare for the loading of the goods, supervise the loading process and get the Bill of Loading, which will be issued within the period of allowed in the letter of credit.

In the cases of CIF, the exporter will have to pay for the sea bill and make sure whether they make insurance for your goods, to be in order to receive the correct bill of lading and bill of insurance at a rapid speed. If these documents cannot be provided in time by the exporter, *the exporter will shoulder the obligation for compensating for the losses of the importer*[16].

◇ Documents and payment

Presentation of documents is very important in the process of documentary credit operation because it will lead to the final settlement of the credit. Therefore, after shipment is made, the exporter should present to *the negotiating bank*[17] the documents within the time specified by the L/C. All the documents not only must be processed in accordance with the L/C terms, but also be completed with absolute accuracy and clarity. The documents generally include commercial invoice, bill of lading, insurance policy and packing list, etc. If the documents presented *strictly comply with*[18] the details in the L/C, the exporter will receive payment from the bank.

Import Procedure

The performance of an import contract is closely related to export procedure. It generally includes the following procedures: letter of credit, shipment and insurance, document examination and payment, customs clearance, taking delivery and inspection etc.

◇ Letter of credit

If L/C is requested by the relevant parties as a means of payment, the importer should open the L/C in time in favor of the exporter. The L/C application should be made to fit the sales contract terms. Any discrepancy will lead to *the amendment to the L/C*[19] requested by the exporter. If such a request is made according to the contract terms, the applicant should apply to *the L/C issuing bank*[20] for amendments. If the amendment request is due to some reasons from the exporter such as the *delayed delivery*[21], it is necessary for the importer to decide whether he can accept the request. If he agrees, he might ask the exporter to pay the amendment fee.

◇ Shipment and insurance

FOB or FAC trade terms are generally used in import contracts. Therefore, it is the importer who must contact at his expense for shipment. After receiving the exporter's notification of being ready for the goods, the importer should book shipping space and effect shipment and at the same time, keep the exporter informed of the progress to facilitate smooth delivery of the goods.

Under FOB, FCA, CFR and CPT terms, the cargo insurance should be effected by the importer, who should ask the exporter to advise the shipment in time *so that the goods can be covered by insurance without delay*[22].

◇ Document examination and payment

When L/C is used, the exporter will present to the negotiating bank the relevant document required by L/C to get payment after the shipment is made. In consequence, the documents will be mailed to the issuing bank to ask for payment or acceptance. Under *documentary collection*[23], even though both of the negotiation bank and the issuing bank have examined the documents, the importer himself should examine the documents carefully to confirm if they meet the requirements of the sales contract before making payment. If the acceptance is due, payment should be made in *the pre-agreed manner*[24].

◇ Customs Clearance

The imported goods must go through customs, and therefore, the importer should submit some documents like invoice, B/L, inspection certificate etc. If necessary, the importer needs to carry out all *customs formalities*[25] for the transit of the goods through any other country. The customs will check the goods against the documents to see whether they match.

◇ Taking delivery and inspection

With the shipping documents, the importer can now take delivery of the goods from the carrier. Then, inspection should be carried out to confirm if the goods are up to the standard set in the sales contract. *If there is any inconformity, such as weight shortage or inferior quality, the importer should make claims against the exporter or other parties concerned for* compensation[26].

 **Notes**

1. perform their rights and obligation：履行权利和义务
2. transfer the property in the goods：转交商品所有权
3. take delivery of：收货
4. Although within some countries, commercial credit such as open account, remittance, D/A is commonly used for the payment and settlement, L/C is still asked for payment by Chinese traders due to its safety：虽然很多国家会使用到诸如未结清账目、汇付、承兑交单等付款方式，但在中国，贸易商们还是因为信用证的安全性原因多采用此付款方式
5. under L/C payment terms：在信用证的付款方式条款下
6. cargo readiness：货物准备就绪
7. customs clearance：报关
8. stipulated delivery time：规定的交货期
9. smooth the transaction：使交易顺利进行
10. expedite the opening of L/C：加速信用证开立
11. consistent with：与……一致
12. proceed to：前往，转入
13. prior to：在……之前
14. commercial invoice, export license, copy of sales contract and inspection certificates：商业发票、出口许可证、销售合同复印件和检验证书
15. book the shipping space：预定舱位
16. the exporter will shoulder the obligation for compensating for the losses of the importer：出口商将对赔偿进口商的损失负责
17. the negotiating bank：议付行
18. strictly comply with：严格遵从
19. the amendment to the L/C：修改信用证
20. the L/C issuing bank：信用证开证行
21. delayed delivery：交货期延误
22. So that the goods can be covered by insurance without delay：以便货物可以立即投保
23. documentary collection：跟单托收
24. the pre-agreed manner：预先约定的方式
25. customs formalities：报关单
26. If there is any inconformity, such as weight shortage or inferior quality, the

importer should make claims against the exporter or other parties concerned for compensation：如果有任何的不一致，诸如重量短缺或质量低劣，进口商应该向出口商或相关方提出投诉，要求赔偿

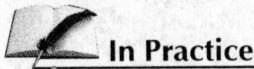 In Practice

> Questions Based on the Text

I. Decide whether the following statements are true or false according to the text.
1. In import and export trade, the basic obligation for the seller is only to provide the buyer with the goods which comply with the requirements in the contract. (   )
2. Under L/C payment terms, the exporter can ship the goods before the opening of the L/C. (   )
3. In the cases of FOB, the exporter will have to book the shipping space and pay for the insurance premium. (   )
4. If there is any amendment to the L/C, the importer can ask the exporter to pay the amendment fee. (   )
5. The importer may refuse to pay if there are discrepancies in the negotiation documents. (   )
6. The exporter can present to the issuing bank the relevant document required to get payment before the shipment is made. (   )
7. For T/T payment terms, the B/L, commercial invoice and packing list should be sent to the buyer through the bank for payment. (   )
8. For unacceptable clauses in an L/C, the seller should contact the issuing bank directly for amendments. (   )

II. Answer these questions according to the text.
1. Please describe briefly the procedures of performing a CIF export contract under L/C payment terms.
2. What should the exporter do if there are discrepancies between the L/C and the sales contract?
3. Why is it important for the exporter to check the L/C against the sales contract carefully after receipt of the L/C?
4. What are the main negotiation documents for L/C payment?
5. What does the import procedure generally include?

Business Vocabulary and Useful Expressions

III. Translate the following terms.
1. take delivery of _____
2. the property in the goods _____
3. customs clearance _____
4. export license _____
5. the negotiating bank _____
6. compensate for _____
7. 报关单 _____
8. 履行权利和义务 _____
9. 货物准备就绪 _____
10. 加速信用证开立 _____
11. 跟单托收 _____
12. 重量短缺 _____

IV. Fill in the blanks with words or phrases given below. Change the form where necessary.

| property | delivery | remittance | readiness | expedite |

1. Please take _____ of the goods at the station next Friday.
2. All her luggage was in _____ for the trip.
3. We assure you that we shall do our utmost to _____ shipment.
4. After his death, his _____ was shared between his children.
5. A telegraphic transfer is the quickest and most efficient _____ method available.

| prescribe | application | amendment | discrepancy | inconformity |

6. He had contributed his lifetime to the pure theory of law, although his viewpoints about law were _____.
7. I didn't receive an acknowledgement of my _____.
8. The _____ to L/C will lead to the delay of the delivery.
9. We must bear in mind the possible _____ between the effect desired and the effect produced.
10. What punishment does the law _____ for corruption?

Chapter 4
International Trade Procedure

> proceed to   consistent with   compensate for   without delay   inferior quality

11. I have therefore irrevocably decided to _____ initial the agreement.
12. She was _____ the loss of her arm in the accident.
13. What you say now is not _____ what you said last week.
14. All these measures must be carried through _____.
15. Our customers are complaining of the _____ of our products.

> ### Workshop

V. Sentence completion with words and phrases given below, two of them are not available.

> present to   open the L/C   under   cargo readiness   the shipping documents   covered   meet the requirements   in conformity with   make claims against   documentations

1. Without _____, the importer cannot take delivery of the goods from the carrier.
2. After signing a contract, the importer should _____ in favor of the exporter.
3. Under CFR, the importer should ask the exporter to advise the shipment in time so that the goods can be _____ by insurance without delay.
4. After shipment, the exporter will _____ the negotiating bank the relevant documents to get payment.
5. Most of the import transactions in this country are _____ CIF term.
6. Under documentary collection, the importer himself should examine the documents presented by the exporter to confirm if they _____ of the sales contract.
7. The import inspection is always taken to confirm if the goods are _____ the terms stipulated in the sales contract. Should any problem occurs, the importer need to the relevant parties immediately.
8. _____ should be completed by the exporter with absolute accuracy and clarity.

> ### Case Study

Shanghai Wonder Industrial Co., Ltd, which has exported ICE-CREAM

MACHINES for many years. It received an irrevocable sight L/C from the importer. The L/C required that the latest shipment date was 10th March 2013. Because of lack of shipping space, Shanghai Wonder could not ship the goods on time and asked the importer to extend the shipment date to the 28th March 2013 and to extend the expiry date of the L/C accordingly. The importer replied to accept the changes with a phone call. Shanghai Wonder then arranged the shipment on the 25th March and submitted the documents for negotiation on the 26th March, but was rejected by the bank.

Is the bank right in doing so? Why?

Chapter 5

Commodity Terms in International Trade

1. Name of Commodity

Commodities are goods and services that are commercially bought and sold, including all manner of goods and services that might be bought or sold as part of a *single transaction*[1].

The orange juice on your breakfast table, the gas in your car, the meat on your dinner plate, and the cotton in your shirt are all traditional examples of commodities, but foreign currencies, *emissions credits*[2], bandwidth, and certain financial instruments also belong to today's commodity markets.

When we do international trade, *we pay for what we get or get paid for what we provide*[3]. The things for which money is paid are goods and services. In our course, we mainly discuss trade in goods, which is also called *visible trade*[4].

The Importance of the Name of Commodity

In the international sale of goods, the sellers and buyers are located in different countries. Generally, only after sales contracts have been concluded, the sellers begin to prepare and deliver goods. In another word, the buyers are usually *unable to see the actual goods delivered until they arrive at the port of destination*[5].

They only *ascertain the subject matter of the transaction by means of some necessary descriptions of goods which they order*[6]. The description of goods generally consists of the name and quality of goods. The name of commodity is regarded as the *major term*[7] and is an *integral part*[8] of a sales contract.

Commodity name refers to the title or concept of a certain commodity that makes this commodity differ from another one. Commodity name is also referred to the "article" or "item" for contracted subject matter.

The name of commodity, to some extent, represents the general quality a commodity possesses, so in *contract wording*[9], a specific name is suggested to be applied. In the contract, the specific name of the transacted commodity is listed under the heading of "Name of Commodity".

How to Name a Commodity?

When giving a name to a commodity, we should select an internationally recognized one so as to *facilitate the procedures for import and export clearance and tariff reduction*[10]. Here are some common ways to name a commodity.

- *Name after its main usages*[11], for example, washing machine.
- Name after its raw materials or main components, for example, deer antler wine.
- Name after its place of origin, for example, *Brazil barbecue*[12].
- Name after its design or outer shape, for example, high heel shoes.
- Name after its *processing technique*[13], for example, refined oil.
- Name after its inventor, for example, Chanel.

From the point of business, naming a commodity is the first step in any business negotiation. As the basis of a transaction, *it has a bearing on the interests and rights of both importers and exporters*[14]. If the commodities delivered by the seller are not *in strict conformity with*[15] the agreed name of commodity, the buyer *reserves the right to lodge a claim, reject the goods or even cancel the contract*[16].

Therefore, as a main condition of sale, the name of commodity should be clearly stipulated. When giving the name, try to *be specific, practical and realistic*[17] and adopt the widely accepted name agreed by both parties.

◇ Be clear and specific

Each commodity of a transaction should be *legal and uncontroversial*[18]. As there are different ways of naming commodities, the expression of the commodity name must be clear and specific to avoid *vagueness and ambiguity*[19].

For example, the name "red wine" sounds too general as there are many different kinds of red wine in the market. In addition, the same type red wine produced in different places may differ in quality and taste. Obviously, as a commodity name, "*Cabernet Sauvignon*[20]" is much better than "red wine".

◇ Be practical and realistic

Any name of commodity stipulated in the contract must comply with the goods that the buyer requires and the seller is able to produce or supply. *Unnecessary modifiers*[21] or *exaggerated descriptions*[22] should not be used.

Take "perfect *mild steel*[23]" for example. Mild steel is the steel with less than 0.15% carbon. The restrictive word "perfect" in the name of commodity "perfect mild steel" is an unnecessary modifier because it is very hard for the exporter to execute the requirement of "perfect".

◇ Adopt widely accepted names

Sometimes, a commodity has different names in different areas. To avoid possible disputes in the future, the name of commodity in the contract should *bear common interpretation by the exporter and the importer*[24]. When naming new products or translating product names, you should try to adopt widely accepted names in the world. For example, "*filet steak*" *is a steak cut of beef taken from the smaller end of the tenderloin*[25], which is very famous and accepted by the people all over the world.

◇ Select an appropriate commodity name

To facilitate importing and reduce customs duties, experts suggest selecting an appropriate name for your commodity. In international trade, *customs tariff*[26] can be further reduced for some commodities than others. For example, "*robot riser*[27]" is auxiliary equipment for robot. With regard to customs tariff, "robot risers" and "risers" will be dealt with in a totally different way. Therefore, choosing an appropriate name as the name of commodity in the contract can be beneficial to both the exporter and the importer.

Notes

1. single transaction：单笔交易
2. emissions credits：排放信用
3. When we do international trade, we pay for what we get or get paid for what we provide：我们在进行国际贸易时,我们为获得的商品付款或者让买家为我们提供的产品付款
4. visible trade：有形贸易
5. unable to see the actual goods delivered until they arrive at the port of destination：在货物到达目的港之前,无法见到交付的现货
6. ascertain the subject matter of the transaction by means of some necessary

descriptions of goods which they order：通过对订购货物的一些必要描述来确认交易中的重要事项

7. major term：主要条款
8. integral part：重要部分；不可缺少的部分
9. contract wording：合同措辞
10. facilitate the procedures for import and export clearance and tariff reduction：有助于进出口贸易的报关清关及关税减免
11. Name after its main usages：以其主要用途来命名
12. Brazil barbecue：巴西烤肉
13. processing technique：生产工艺
14. It has a bearing on the interests and rights of both importers and exporters：它关系着进口商和出口商的利益和权利
15. in strict conformity with：与……严格一致
16. The buyer reserves the right to lodge a claim, reject the goods or even cancel the contract：买家可保留索赔、拒货、甚至取消订单的权利
17. be specific, practical and realistic：具体、实用、实际
18. legal and uncontroversial：合法和无可争议的
19. vagueness and ambiguity：含糊不清、模棱两可
20. Cabernet Sauvignon：赤露珠(法国红酒品牌)
21. unnecessary modifiers：不必要的修饰词
22. exaggerated descriptions：夸张的描述
23. mild steel：低碳钢
24. bear common interpretation by the exporter and the importer：符合进出口商双方的共同理解
25. "Filet steak" is a steak cut of beef taken from the smaller end of the tenderloin："菲力牛排"是从牛的腰部嫩肉割下的牛排
26. customs tariff：关税
27. robot riser：机器人底座

In Practice

➢ Questions Based on the Text

I. Decide whether the following statements are true or false according to the text.

1. A book you bought from the bookshop is a commodity.　　　　　(　　)

2. In international trade, both the exporter and the importer must see the commodity before delivery.   (   )
3. The description of goods generally consists of the name and quantity of commodity.   (   )
4. Hand-woven carpet is named after its processing technique.   (   )
5. Glass cup is named after its usages.   (   )
6. The word of "pure" in the name of commodity "Pure cotton Jacket" is unnecessary modifier because it is difficult for the seller to fulfill the contract.   (   )
7. When naming new products, try to adopt a name of commodity widely accepted internationally.   (   )
8. All the commodities often have the same customs tariff in one country.   (   )

II. Answer these questions according to the text.
1. What is a commodity?
2. Is Euro a commodity?
3. Why is the name of commodity very important?
4. What may the importer do if the commodity delivered is not the one agreed by both parties?
5. How should people select an appropriate commodity name?

> **Business Vocabulary and Useful Expressions**

III. Translate the following terms.
1. name of commodity _____
2. foreign currency _____
3. port of destination _____
4. import and export clearance _____
5. single transaction _____
6. in strict conformity with _____
7. 夸张的描述 _____
8. 保留权利 _____
9. 商务洽谈 _____
10. 索赔 _____
11. 避免争端 _____
12. 加速进程 _____

IV. Fill in the blanks with words or phrases given below. Change the form where necessary.

> component   commodity   financial   negotiate   transact

1. _____ prices remain stable and there are plenty of goods on the market.
2. The company has enormous _____ firepower.
3. Usually models have many _____ parts, each to be made separately.
4. We use e-commerce to market or _____ our products and services.
5. I managed to _____ successfully with the experienced negotiator.

> refine   specific   realistic   ambiguity   exaggerate

6. Would you please give me _____ instructions for this machine?
7. The message was misunderstood because of its _____.
8. Don't _____, I was only two minutes late, not twenty minutes.
9. Police have to be _____ about violent crime and deal with it.
10. _____ sugars are absorbed into the bloodstream very quickly.

> be concluded   be regarded as   name after   have a bearing on   in conformity with

11. The transaction will _____ within the month.
12. Our sandwich was _____ a man named Sandwich.
13. She's indifferent to anything that doesn't _____ her.
14. It _____ a natural behavior that a man helps the old walk across the road.
15. The plan was made _____ their views.

➢ Workshop

V. Look at the commodity pictures below and choose the right answer.

Ginseng capsules

1. Ginseng capsules are named after _____.
   a. its main ingredients
   b. its raw materials
   c. its processing technique

Chapter 5
Commodity Terms in International Trade

(Continued)

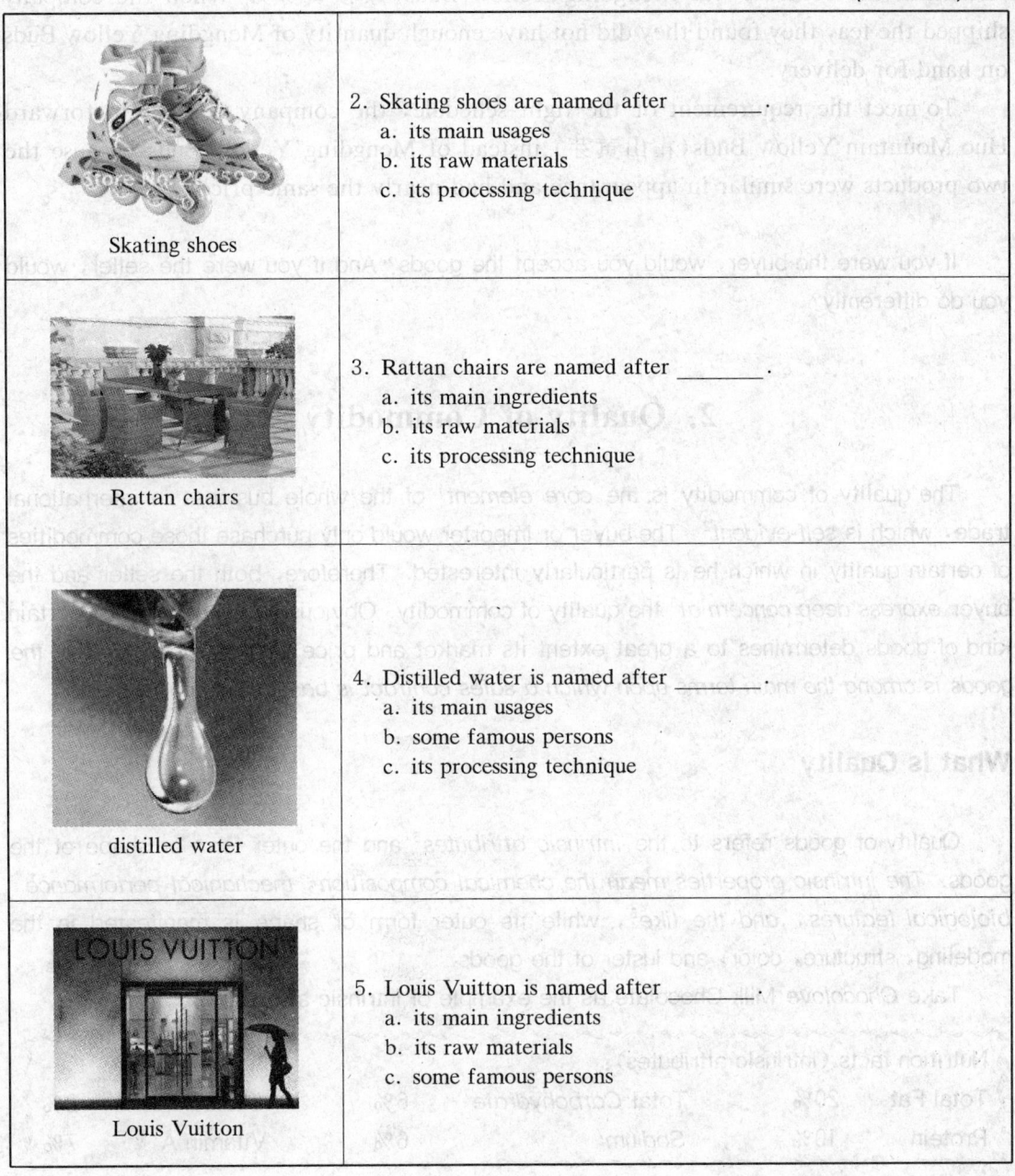

2. Skating shoes are named after _____.
   a. its main usages
   b. its raw materials
   c. its processing technique

3. Rattan chairs are named after _____.
   a. its main ingredients
   b. its raw materials
   c. its processing technique

4. Distilled water is named after _____.
   a. its main usages
   b. some famous persons
   c. its processing technique

5. Louis Vuitton is named after _____.
   a. its main ingredients
   b. its raw materials
   c. some famous persons

> **Case Study**

China Hexin Green Tea Industry Co., Ltd signed a sales contract to export Yellow Buds, which is among the top ten brands of Chinese tea. The name of commodity as written in the contract was Mengding Yellow Buds(蒙顶黄芽). When the company shipped the tea, they found they did not have enough quantity of Mengding Yellow Buds on hand for delivery.

To meet the requirement of the tight schedule, the company decided to forward Huo Mountain Yellow Buds(霍山黄芽) instead of Mengding Yellow Buds because the two products were similar in appearance and had nearly the same price.

If you were the buyer, would you accept the goods? And if you were the seller, would you do differently?

2. Quality of Commodity

The quality of commodity is the *core element*[1] of the whole business in international trade, which is *self-evident*[2]. The buyer or importer would only purchase those commodities of certain quality in which he is particularly interested. Therefore, both the seller and the buyer *express deep concern at*[3] the quality of commodity. Obviously, the quality of a certain kind of goods determines to a great extent its market and price. Thus, *the quality of the goods is among the main terms upon which a sales contract is based and constructed*[4].

What Is Quality

Quality of goods refers to the *intrinsic attributes*[5] and the outer form or shape of the goods. *The intrinsic properties mean the chemical composition, mechanical performance, biological features, and the like*[6], while its outer form or shape is manifested in the modeling, structure, color, and luster of the goods.

Take *Chocolove* Milk Chocolate as the example of intrinsic attributes.

Nutrition facts (intrinsic attributes):
Total Fat	20%	Total *Carbohydrate*[7]	6%	*Cholesterol*[7]	8%
Protein	10%	*Sodium*[7]	6%	Vitamin A	7%

How to Determine Quality

Since quality plays an important role in the sales of a product, transferring the information of quality in a right way to customers is vital. However, international transactions cover a wide range of commodities and their features *differ from one another*[8]. Different products may require different ways to determine their quality. In general, there are three ways of identifying the quality of commodity.

Quality Stipulations	
Categories	Types
Sale by Description	Sale by Specification
	Sale by Grade
	Sale by Standard
	Sale by Brand Name or Trade Mark
	Sale by Place of Origin
	Sale by Description or Illustrations
Sale by Sample	Sale by Seller's Sample
	Sale by Buyer's Sample
	Sale by Counter Sample
Sale by Actual Commodity/ Sale by Actual Quality	

Sale by Description

In foreign trade, most commodities are suitable for sale by description which can be subdivided into six kinds: sale by specification, sale by grade, sale by standard, sale by brand name or *trade mark*[9], sale by place of origin, *sale by descriptions or illustrations*[10]. Sale by description is the way of expressing quality with words and illustrations.

◇ Sale by specification

Defining quality by specification is widely used in international trade as the way of determining commodity quality by specification is simple, accurate and convenient. It refers to certain indicators which express the quality of the commodities, such as composition, content, purity, size, length, etc. Different indicators will be applied to different products; some examples are as the following:

The quality of crispy date is expressed by the *ingredients content*[11].

Ingredients:
Red date[12], Refined vegetable oil, Honey, *Acesulfame-k*[12]

The quality of LED display is expressed by *technical parameters*[13].

> Parameters:
> Life span: ≥50 thousand hours   Brightness: ≥3000 cd/m²
> Display size: m(width)× m(height)   *Perspective Level*[14]: 120°, vertical: 120°

◇ **Sale by grade**

Sometimes, the same kind of commodities might also be classified into different grades, such as Grade A, Grade B, Grade C, according to different qualities, appearances, weights, compositions, etc. It is better to state the quality by grade after a grade is given, which is simplified for both the exporter and the importer.

For example, White Crystal Sugar is classified as four grades: *Refined Grade*[15], Superior Grade, Grade 1 and Grade 2.

Items	Refined Grade	Superior Grade	Grade 1	Grade 2
Sucrose Content[16] (%)	99.8	99.7	99.6	99.5
Reducing Sugar[16] (%)	0.03	0.04	0.1	0.15
Conductometric Ash[16] (%)	0.02	0.04	0.1	0.13

Of course, to avoid misunderstanding and the subsequent disputes, the seller and the buyer are supposed to have *reached a consensus on the classification implication of grades in advance*[17].

◇ **Sale by standard**

The specifications or grades become standards when they are laid down and proclaimed in a unified way[18]. They have *legal effects*[19] and are binding upon both the exporter and the importer. A standard is an *established norm*[20] or requirement. There are various levels of standards that are formulated by governments or by *commercial organizations*[21] formally.

For example, in international agricultural and *by-product market*[22], there is a commonly adopted standard, i.e. fair average quality (short for F. A. Q.). It refers to the average quality level of export commodity within a certain period of time.

◇ **Sale by brand name or trade mark**

Brand is the name to identify a product from a certain manufacturer, which is the image for the customers to distinguish the product from other similar ones. Typical examples are as

follows:
- Apple iPhone 5s
- HP (Hewlett-Packard) Printer
- Dior Perfume

Trade mark is a legal term, which includes all those words, symbols or marks that are legally registered for use by a single company[23]. It is a recognizable sign, design or expression located on a package, a label or on the product itself. For example, the *Burberry check pattern*[24] is a registered trademark of Burberry Ltd.

◇ Sale by name of origin

Some products, especially native products, are often very famous and well-known by the place of origin. Sale by name of origin is more suitable for agricultural products or by-products. The products are more welcome whenever their places of origin are mentioned, such as pears from Dangshan, porcelain from Jingdezhen, crabs from Ynagcheng Lake etc.

◇ Sale by description or illustration

Some products with complicated structure and various features of function, such as *technological instruments, electric machines and transportation tools*[25] etc. are very hard to be expressed with several simple indicators. Therefore, specific descriptions are necessary for stating the quality. Sometimes pictures, photos, charts, drawings, etc. must also be provided. In order to protect their benefits, some buyers often require the seller to include the *quality assurance clauses* and *technical service clauses*[26] into the contract. For example, "HP ENVY 14-k001tx Sleekbook Product, quality and data to be strictly in conformity with the instructions attached."

Sale by Sample

Sale by sample is a sale in which the buyer purchases goods under an agreed condition that goods sold are as good as one shown to the buyer as a sample. A sample is a product, often taken out from a whole lot of consignment or specially designed and processed. Samples can be provided by either the seller or the buyer. According to different cases, it can be divided into three types.

◇ Sale by seller's sample

In this case, the seller shall provide a *representative sample*[27] which will possess the moderate quality among a large quantity of the actual commodities. Meantime, a duplicate sample is always kept by the seller for later reference. In the contract, it should be clearly stipulated that quality is "as per seller's sample" and the quality of the actual goods should conform to that of the sample.

◇ Sale by buyer's sample

Samples can also be provided by the buyer. They are given as the quality standard for the commodities to be provided and shipped by the seller. Therefore, when a sale is made based on the sample provided by the buyer, the seller has to study the samples thoroughly to make sure that all details are covered. If the quality of the goods delivered is not identical with the sample, *the buyer is entitled to claim compensation for losses or reject the goods*[28].

◇ Sale by *counter sample*

Sometimes, a sale made by buyer's sample is hard for the seller to manage due to raw material supply, processing technique or equipment available. The seller may reproduce the buyer's sample, i. e. *counter sample*[29], and send it back to the buyer as a type sample. After the buyer has confirmed the counter sample, sale by the buyer's sample is changed into sale by the seller's counter sample.

Sale by Actual Quality

Sale by actual quality is a sale made on the basis that the buyer has inspected the goods and intended to buy them as a result of this inspection. It is usually displayed at the trade fair or the goods *at the premises*[30]. After the buyer and the seller conclude a deal, the seller shall deliver the goods that have been examined.

This method is of special necessity for particular goods such as jewels, famous paintings and auctions etc.

Notes

1. core element：核心元素

Chapter 5
Commodity Terms in International Trade

2. self-evident：不证自明的
3. express deep concern at：对……表现出深切的关心
4. The quality of the goods is among the main terms upon which a sales contract is based and constructed：商品的质量是销售合同主要条款的基础
5. intrinsic attributes：本质属性
6. The intrinsic properties mean the chemical composition, mechanical performance, biological features, and the like：本质性质就是指化学成分、机械性能、生物特征等等
7. Carbohydrate, Cholesterol, Sodium：碳水化合物,胆固醇,元素钠 Na
8. differ from one another：各不相同
9. trade mark：商标
10. sale by descriptions or illustrations：依据描述或插图说明销售
11. ingredients content：成分含量
12. Red date, Acesulfame：红枣,乙酰舒泛
13. technical parameters：技术参数
14. Perspective Level：视觉水平
15. Refined Grade：精制级别
16. Sucrose Content, Reducing Sugar, Conductometric Ash：蔗糖、还原糖、电导灰分
17. reached a consensus on the classification implication of grades in advance：对级别的分类含义提前达成共识
18. The specifications or grades become standards when they are laid down and proclaimed in a unified way：当以一种标准统一的方式对规格或级别进行制定时,它们就变成了标准
19. legal effects：法律效力
20. established norm：制定的标准
21. commercial organizations：商业组织
22. by-product market：副产品市场
23. Trade mark is a legal term, which includes all those words, symbols or marks that are legally registered for use by a single company：商标是指一个公司注册登记使用的包括所有的文字、符号或者标记在内的有法律效力的标志
24. Burberry check pattern：巴宝莉的格子图案
25. Some products with complicated structure and various features of function, such as technological instruments, electric machines and transportation tools：有些产品具有复杂的结构和不同的特征功能,比如像技术设备、电子器械和交通工具等
26. quality assurance clauses and technical service clauses：质量保证条款和技术服务条款
27. representative sample：具有代表性的样品
28. The buyer is entitled to claim compensation for losses or reject the goods：买家有权

对损失提出赔偿或者拒绝接受货物
29. counter sample：相对样本
30. at the premises：在交易场所

 **In Practice**

➢ **Questions Based on the Text**

I. Decide whether the following statements are true or false according to the text.
  1. Quality of goods means theouter form or shape of the goods.   (　)
  2. In international trade, superior quality always enjoys good market.   (　)
  3. The way of determining the quality of the commodities by specifications is called sale by specification, which is comparatively convenient and accurate.   (　)
  4. The quality of electric products is expressed by ingredients contents.   (　)
  5. The quality of the goods can be known by simply stating its grade. However, the seller and the buyer should reach a consensus on the "grades".   (　)
  6. F.A.Q is one of examples of sale by standard.   (　)
  7. For some products, their qualities are usually expressed by indicating the names of origin as the places are very beautiful.   (　)
  8. Sale by actual quality is usually applied to the trade of some goods such as jewels, famous paintings and auctions etc.   (　)

II. Answer these questions according to the text.
  1. What is quality?
  2. Why is the quality of commodity very important?
  3. How many ways can be used to identify the qunlity commodity?
  4. What is a troule maik?
  5. What should the seller do if the sample is proridecl by the buyer?

➢ **Business Vocabulary and Useful Expressions**

III. Translate the following terms.
  1. chemical composition ＿＿＿＿＿
  2. intrinsic attributes ＿＿＿＿＿
  3. sale bydescription or illustration ＿＿＿＿＿

4. trade mark _____
5. reach a consensus on _____
6. commercial organizations _____
7. 不证自明的 _____
8. 成分含量 _____
9. 技术参数 _____
10. 副产品市场 _____
11. 相对样本 _____
12. 质量保证条款 _____

IV. Fill in the blanks with words or phrases given below. Change the form where necessary.

| purchase   determine   intrinsic   illustration   appearance |

1. The house is the most expensive _____ I have ever made.
2. It is hard to distinguish between extrinsic and _____ motivation.
3. We should not judge a person by his _____.
4. He used photographs as _____ for his talk.
5. She is _____ to do regardless of all consequences.

| subsequent   proclaim   commercial   identify   consignment |

6. I was officially hooked, and began to publicly _____ my support.
7. Our agent _____ will wait on you next Monday.
8. W.P.A plus Risk of Breakage suits your _____.
9. Reading this book, we can _____ with the main character's struggle.
10. The problem will be discussed at length in _____ chapters.

| as per   be entitled to   reach a consensus on
  express deep concern at   differ from |

11. The members have not _____ some issues.
12. It is for this reason that we quarrel over the question, because our scales of values _____ one another.
13. We _____ the news that your country has been struck by an earthquake.
14. You may _____ reclaim some of the tax you paid last year.
15. Will you please send me the books _____ list attached?

➤ Workshop

V. Look at the commodity pictures below and choose the right ways of identifying the quality of commodity.

> A. Sale by specification B. Sale by grade
> C. Sale by standard D. Sale by brand name or trade mark
> E. Sale by place of origin F. Sale by description or illustrations

Quick Details
INGREDIENTS: WATER,
BIFIDA FERMENT
LYSATE, GLYCERIN,
ALCOHOL DIMETHICONE

Sale by _____

Quick Details
BRAND NAME: NEWWAY
USAGE: SHOPPING BAG
FOR FOOD, RICE,
GRAIN.

Sale by _____

Quick Details
STYLE: FRESH
TYPE: TABLE EGG
GRADE: JIADUO-14

Sale by _____

Quick Details
TYPE: FOOD
TASTE: SOUR
PLACE OF ORIGIN:
JAPAN

Sale by _____

➤ Case Study

Manly entered Bradford's store and offered to sell him some cloves, at the same time exhibiting him a sample. The sample shown was of the very best quality. Bradford agreed to purchase six hundred and two pounds at $1.50 a pound. When the consignment arrived, Bradford found that it was not Cayenne cloves but a much more inferior quality. Thereupon, Bradford brought this action to recover damages.

Manly contended that he had warranted, neither expressly nor by implication that the consignment would be like the sample shown. Bradford said: "The fair import of the exhibition of a sample is that the article proposed to be sold is like that which is shown as a parcel of the article".

If you were Mr. Chief Justice, whom will you give judgment to? Why?

3. Quantity of Commodity

A business deal cannot be completed without *caring for*[1] the quantity of the goods sold or bought. The quantity of commodity is a major indispensable clause in a contract. *According to the United Nations Convention on Contract for the International Sale of Goods (CISG), the buyer may take delivery or has the right to reject the goods if their quantity delivered is less than agreed upon*[2]. The buyer is also entitled to reject the whole lot or that portion of the goods *excessive in quantity*[3]. Therefore, it is very important for both sides to stipulate the quantity clauses correctly. The business laws of certain countries stipulate that the quantity of goods delivered should *be identical to*[4] that called for in the contract.

Many countries may adopt different systems of weights and measures, the units and ways of quantity calculation are varied as different products have different characteristics.

The Systems of Weights and Measures

◇ Metric system

The metric system is an internationally agreed *decimal system*[5] of measurement introduced by France in 1799. Primary units under this system are kilogram (kg), meter (m), square meter (sq. m) and liter (l). Some other *derived units*[6] are metric ton (M/T), kilometer (km) and so on. This system is widely used by European continent and many other countries.

◇ International system

This system is the modern form of the metric system and is the world's most widely used system of measurement in both everyday commerce and science. Its fundamental units include kilogram, meter, second, and so on. This is China's legal metrical system.

◇ British system

British system was mostly used in the British Commonwealth and the former British

Empire. Under this system, primary units are pound and yard. By the late 20th century, *announcement of abandoning*[7] this system has been made by Britain since it has been a member of EU (*European Union*[8]). Now it adopts the metric system. However, some imperial units are still used in the United Kingdom and Canada.

◇ American system

It is also called the United States customary system of units, commonly used in the United States. Since the system developed from British system, its primary units are the same as the ones of British system, i.e. pound and yard. But there are differences in some derived units.

For example, the British system's *long ton*[9], L/T equals to 2200 pounds while the US system's *short ton*[10], S/T equals to 2000 pounds.

Quantity Units

There are two categories of metric units, which are used to show the quantity of commodity in international trade. One is the metric unit, including weight, length, area, volume and capacity; the other is number, including some customary units such as *dozen*, *gross*, *great gross*, *ream*, and some packing units like *barrel*, *bale*, *etc*[11].

	Units of Measurement		Products
Metric unit	Weight	gram(g), kilogram(kg), ounce(oz), pound (1b), metric ton(M/T), long ton, short ton, etc.	mineral products, agricultural and by-products such as wool, cotton, grains and ore
	Length	meter(m), centimeter(cm), foot(ft), yard(yd)	textile products, metal cords, electric wires, ropes
	Area	square meter(sq m), square foot(sq ft), square yard(sq yd), etc.	glass, textile products
	Volume	cubic meter(cu m), cubic centimeter(cu cm), cubic foot(cu ft), cubic yard(cu yd), etc.	timber/wood, chemical gases
	Capacity	Liter(l), gallon(gal), pint(pt), bushel(bu)	grain, petroleum/oil
Number	Number	piece(pc), package(pkg), pair, set, dozen (doz), gross(gr), ream(rm), etc.	industrial products and general products such as ready-made clothes, stationery, paper, toys

Methods for Calculating Weight

In international trade, many products are measured by weight, such as rice, salt and oil etc. According to general commercial practices and rules, weight is usually calculated in the following ways.

◇ *Gross weight*[12]

It refers to the weight of the cargo itself plus the tare, i.e., the weight of the cargo plus the weight of the packing material. It is suitable for commodities with low price or low freight.

◇ *Net weight*[13]

Net weight is used widely in international trade. The weight is calculated by net weight unless otherwise stated in the contract. It means the weight of the product itself, and the tare *is not counted in*[14]:

Net weight = Gross weight − Tare

The following are some methods of calculating tare.
- *Actual tare*[15] or real tare: The actual weight of the package.
- *Average tare*[16]: The weight is calculated on the basis of the average by selecting some of them and working out the average when the packages are in the same sizes.
- *Customary tare*[17]: This is suitable for standardized package. The weight of the package is known to everyone and *universally acknowledged*[18]. It is unnecessary to weigh.
- *Computed tare*[19]: The weight of the package is agreed upon by the parties concerned.

Some cargoes, such as *tobacco flakes*, *news reels*[20] whose packages are not convenient to be calculated by net weight, or those, the values of the packing materials are almost the same as the values of the cargoes themselves, such as grain, fodder, etc., are often calculated by gross weight, which is called "*gross for net*[21]" in international trade.

For Example, "Northeast China rice, 1,500M/T, packed in single new gunny bags, 100 kilograms per bag, gross for net."

◇ *Conditional weight*[22]

This kind of calculating method is suitable for those cargoes whose water contents are not stable, such as wool, silk, etc. In order to determine the *moisture contents*[23] accurately, the universal conditional weight is used. Conditional weight equals to dry weight plus standard moisture content:

Conditional weight = Dry weight + Standard moisture content

◇ *Theoretical weight*[24]

Some commodities are of uniform sizes or regular specifications, so the weight of each unit is almost the same. We can get the total weight by multiplying the total number and the weight of each unit, rather than measured actually. Theoretical weight is applicable to commodities such as *galvanized iron*, *tin plate and steel plate*[25].

More or Less Clause[26]

Since the quantity of commodity plays a key role in a contact, the quantity clause in a sales contract should always be stated clearly and correctly. Such expression as "About 100 cubic meters" is not advisable. Here the word "about" may mean 2.5%, 5% or 10%. The *ambiguous wording*[27] will surely give rise to disputes and should be avoided.

However, on the other hand, sometimes it is hard to strictly control the quantity of goods supplied, such as agricultural products and mineral products. Besides, the differences in transport facilities may also lead to the inconsistency between the actual shipped quantity and the contracted quantity. Under such circumstances, more or less clause is often used so that the business can be executed smoothly. In international trade, it is common to allow the seller to deliver the goods with a certain percentage of more or less in quantity accordingly. *It means over-load and under-load are permitted but should not surpass a certain percentage of the stipulated quantity*[28].

For Example, "South America Coffee Bean, 50,000 M/T, 2005 crop. F.A.Q. with 5% more or less both in quantity and amount to be allowed *at the seller's option*[29]."

Under the more or less clause, the payment for the over-load or under-load will be made according to the contract price or at the market price at the time of shipment.

 Notes

1. caring for: 关注；顾忌
2. According to the United Nations Convention on Contract for the International Sale

of Goods (CISG), the buyer may take delivery or has the right to reject the goods if their quantity delivered is less than agreed upon：根据《联合国国际货物买卖合同公约》，在货物数量少于之前商定的情况下，买家可以接受货物，也有权力拒绝接受货物

3. excessive in quantity：超量
4. be identical to：保持一致
5. decimal system：十进制
6. derived units：导出单位
7. announcement of abandoning：废弃宣告
8. European Union：欧洲联盟
9. long ton：长吨
10. short ton：短吨
11. dozen, gross, great gross, ream, and some packing units like barrel, bale, etc：打、罗、大罗、令和一些如桶、捆等包装单位
12. gross weight：毛重
13. net weight：净重
14. is not counted in：不包括在……里面
15. actual tare：实际皮重
16. average tare：平均皮重
17. customary tare：习惯皮重
18. computed tare：推定皮重
19. universally acknowledged：普遍公认
20. tobacco flakes, news reels：烟叶、新闻胶片
21. gross for net：以毛作净
22. conditional weight：公量
23. moisture contents：水分含量
24. theoretical weight：理论重量
25. galvanized iron, tin plate and steel plate：镀锌铁、镀锡钢片、钢板
26. more or less clause：溢短装条款
27. ambiguous wording：含糊不清的措辞
28. It meansover-load and under-load are permitted but should not surpass a certain percentage of the stipulated quantity：它指允许过量发货或者发货数量不足，但是不能超过规定数量的一定百分比
29. at the seller's option：由卖方决定

In Practice

➤ Questions Based on the Text

I. Decide whether the following statements are true or false according to the text.

1. If the seller delivers a quantity of goods greater than that provided for in the contract, the buyer doesn't have the right to refuse to take delivery of the whole lot. ( )
2. Different countries use different measurement systems. ( )
3. "Long ton" in the British system is the same as "short ton" in the US system. ( )
4. Paper can be calculated by thecustomary unit of ream. ( )
5. Gross weight is the sum of total weight of the commodity itself and the tare. ( )
6. Average tare refers to the weight which is calculated on the basis of the average weight of a part of the packages. ( )
7. Under the clause of "Gross for Net", the goods will be priced by their gross weight instead of the net. ( )
8. It is popular to use those uncertain words like about, approximate to define the quantity. ( )

II. Answer these questions according to the text.

1. Why is the quantity of commodity indispensable?
2. Generally, how many systems of weights and measures are there?
3. Which unit of measurement is used for mineral products?
4. What is "Gross for net" in international trade?
5. Will the buyer pay for the over-load under the more or less clause?

➤ Business Vocabulary and Useful Expressions

III. Translate the following terms.

1. at the seller's option _____
2. announcement _____
3. care for _____
4. take delivery _____

Chapter 5
Commodity Terms in International Trade

5. European Union _____
6. gross for net _____
7. 净重 _____
8. 公量 _____
9. 溢短装条款 _____
10. 含糊不清的措辞 _____
11. 短吨 _____
12. 普遍公认 _____

IV. Fill in the blanks with words or phrases given below. Change the form where necessary.

> indispensable   convention   abandon   excessive   barrel

1. Speaking study, diligence is _____.
2. A second major oil shock in 1979, aided by this revolution, sent oil prices up past $40 a _____.
3. The poor little cat has been _____.
4. _____ amounts of this radiation can cause skin cancer in man and damage plant life.
5. His romance and adventure were battering at the _____.

> moisture   inconsistency   theoretical   advisable   percentage

6. It will be _____ for you to drop an acquaintance such as john; he is not a good companion for you.
7. These findings have both _____ and practical applications.
8. The _____ of the world's gross national product represented by their economy was sinking by 10 percent with every decade.
9. Seeds are germinated by warmth and _____.
10. There are a number of _____ in the book.

> be counted in   equal to   be identical to   net weight   be applicable to

11. You are _____ him in position and in money.
12. The _____ of each bag is 5 kg, attached with product label.
13. The terms of the acceptance shall _____ those of the offer.
14. Select relevant part that _____ you.
15. You can take part in these activities in the introduction. These _____ the ticket inside, and still very cost effective.

➤ Workshop

V. Please match the commodities with the proper units of measurement. The first example is given.

A. metric ton(M/T)
B. meter(m)
C. kilogram(kg)
D. cubic meter(cu m)
E. square meter(sq m)
F. liter(l)
G. pair
H. set
I. ream
J. dozen

1. ropes
2. paper
3. oxygen
4. wheat
5. TV
6. silk
7. rice
8. rose
9. shoes
10. olive oil

➤ Case Study

Shandong Cereals, Oils and Foodstuffs Import and Export Corporation exported 5,000M/T rice to South African at the price of UDS $350 per ton, under the clause "5,000M/T, the sellers are allowed to load 5% more or less, the price shall be calculated according to the unit price in the contract". Both the contract and the L/C stipulated that partial shipment was prohibited. When the goods arrived the port of shipment, it was found that 10 tons were damaged by the rain due to improper packing.

The consignor decided that according to the clause agreed, 5% more or less was allowed if the amount didn't exceed the L/C amount. In the end, 4,990M/T rice were delivered to the importer.

Do you think it was reasonable for the consignor to do so? Why?

4. Packing and Marking of Commodity

In international trade, since the distance between exporter and importer is very far, the cargo is shipped thousands of miles away from its origin and moved for many times.

For example, you need to move a cargo from Shanghai to New York. The cargo will be sent by truck to nearest *CFS* (*container freight station*)[1] of your factory, unloading to warehouse, *stuffing into*[2] container, moving to port of shipping, vessel sailing New York on the basis of *direct steamer*[3]. After arriving in port of destination, the cargo will be unloaded in CFS, moving for inspection procedures, and loading to truck after *customs clearance*[4].

In each movement point mentioned above, if the packing of goods is poor, there are chances of damage, while handling with forklift, or other equipments even though proper supervision is available. *Therefore, the cargo should be taken every necessary step from the design of packaging to the choice of transport to avoid any risk in international trade*[5].

Besides, packing is one of the important ways to realize the value of commodities, which can prettify, identify and market commodities. Packing can be divided into transport packing and selling packing according to their different functions for commodities.

Selling packing[6] is also called inner packing. It is not only designed as a form of protection to reduce the risk of goods being damaged in transit and *prevent pilferage*[7], but also to *promote sales*[8]. Transport packing is also called outer packing that will be mainly discussed.

Types of Transport Packing

When it comes to packing, not all goods are necessarily packed. Generally speaking, cargoes always fall into three groups:
- *Bulk cargoes or cargoes in bulk*[9]: wheat, mineral ore, coal.
- *Nude cargoes*[10]: planks, vehicles, bronze or steel plates or blocks.
- Packed cargoes: all the other cargoes.

The first two groups of cargoes do not need packing while the third group does. For the packed goods, transport packing is mainly to keep the goods *safe and sound*[11] during transportation. It must not only be solid enough to prevent the packed goods from any damage, but be pilferage-proof, easy to store, convenient to load and unload as well.

Transport packing can be categorized into *unit packing*[12] and *collective packing*[13]. The first one is used on the smallest shippable unit of cargo, such as cases, drums, bags and bales, etc. To convenience transportation, unit goods are assembled or consolidated into large containers, which is called collective packing. Pallet, flexible container, and container are the commonly used equipments for collective packing.

Unit Packing

◇ Case

It is an expensive form of packing and is wooden or plastic in structure and of various sizes, including *wooden case*, *crate*, *plastic case and corrugated carton*[14]. This type of packing gives complete protection and lessens pilferage plus an aid to handling, which is used for the goods that cannot be compressed tightly and the other items of expensive equipment. For example, computers.

◇ Drum or cask

It includes *wooden cask*, *iron drum*, *barrel*, *hogshead*, *plastic cask*[15], which is used for the conveyance of liquid or greasy and powdered or granular goods.

◇ Bag

It made of jute, cotton, and plastic, is a cheap form of container and is ideal for a wide of variety of goods, such as fertilizer, flour, chemicals and cement etc.

◇ Bale or bundle

It is *a heap of material pressed together*[16] and tied with rope or metal wire, which is suitable for soft goods, such as, wool, cotton, silk and feather etc.

◇ Crate

It is a form of container halfway between a bale and a case[17]. It often has a bottom and a frame, sometimes open at the top. Crate is built for the lightweight goods of large *cubic capacity*[18] as machinery and some goods that need a special bottom to *facilitate handling*[19].

Collective packing

◇ Pallet

It is a kind of portable platform *intended for*[20] handling, storing, or moving materials. Pallets can move cargos in loads instead of single pieces from one place to another to save time for handling of *separate items*[21].

◇ Flexible container

It is a bag made of fiber with different sizes to hold powdery commodities, like cement, flint and powder rubber etc.

◇ Container

It is a large metal case, of standard shape and size, for transport of goods by road, rail, sea or air. Packing goods in a large container facilitates loading and unloading by mechanical handling.

Marks on Transport Packing

Marks means to have some designs, letters, diagrams and numbers stenciled on the transport packing of cargos to *identify goods and facilitate correct operation*[22]. It is used for understanding the place of origin, for simplifying the examination of documents and for the protection of cargos. According to their functions, marks can be classified into four types: *shipping mark*, *indicative mark*, *warning mark and supplementary mark*[23].

Shipping Mark

It is a type of marking on the shipping packing to facilitate the identification and count of the goods in the process of loading and unloading, shipping and storing. It can also prevent the goods from being wrongly delivered or shipped. Shipping mark often consists of the following four parts:
- Consignee's code: usually the initial or abbreviation of a consignee.
- Destination: the name of the port or place of destination.
- Reference no: the number of the relevant contract, order, invoice.
- Number of package: the consecutive number of each package.

For example, 10 cases of goods will be from Shanghai Beite Co. Ltd to Detroit, the USA, and the number of purchase order is 45002145, in which case the shipping mark may be as follows:

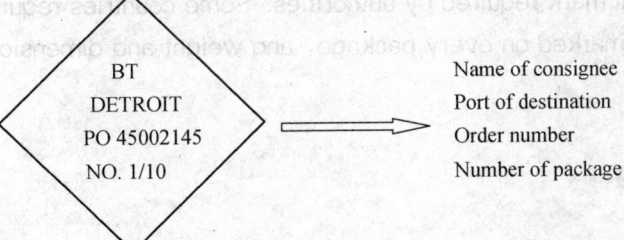

Indicative Mark

Indicative mark is a requirement needing attention for transporting, loading and unloading, storing goods. It is usually marked with pictures and languages, such as FRAGILE, KEEP DRY, THIS WAY UP and CENTRE OF GRAVITY[24].

FRAGILE   KEEP DAY   THIS WAY UP   CENTRE OF GRAVITY

Warning Mark

It can help the persons concerned to *take protective measures to guarantee the good conditions of goods and the life security of people*[25]. It is composed of pictures and phrases printed on the package of the goods by the exporter according to some dangerous characteristics such as INFLAMMABLE, EXPLOSIVE, POISONOUS and RADIOACTIVE[26] products.

INFLAMMABLE   EXPLOSIVEE   POISONOUS   RADIOACTIVE

Supplementary Mark

It is any official mark required by authorities. Some countries require the name of origin of the goods to be marked on every package, and weight and dimensions of the goods may also be required.

Neutral Packing

Neutral packing is a special type of marking rather than a type of packing as its name may indicate. It is the one that *makes no mentions at all*[27] of the name and address of the manufacturer, the origin of country, the trade mark and brand on both outer and inner packages. The purpose of using it by exporters is to break down the tariff and non-tariff barriers of some countries or regions, or *meet the special demand*[28] of the transaction to facilitate the buyer to resell the goods.

It may also help the manufacturers in exporting countries to increase the competitiveness of their products, expand the exports and market profitably in the importing countries.

 Notes

1. CFS (container freight station)：集装箱货物集散站
2. stuffing into：把……装入
3. direct steamer：直达船
4. customs clearance：报关
5. Therefore, the cargo should be taken every necessary step from the design of packaging to the choice of transport to avoid any risk in international trade：因此，为了避免在国际贸易中出现任何危险，货物从包装设计到运输渠道的选择都要采取必要的措施
6. selling packing：销售包装
7. prevent pilferage：防偷盗
8. promote sales：促销
9. bulk cargoes or cargoes in bulk：散装货
10. nude cargoes：裸装货
11. safe and sound：完好无损
12. unit packing：单件包装
13. collective packing：集合包装
14. It is an expensive form of packing and is wooden or plastic in structure and of various sizes, including wooden case, crate, plastic case and corrugated carton：它是一种昂贵的包装形式，是木头或塑料结构的，而且尺寸不一，包括木箱、板条箱、塑料箱和波纹硬纸盒箱
15. wooden cask, iron drum, barrel, hogshead, plastic cask：木桶、铁桶、圆桶、大桶、塑料桶
16. a heap of material pressed together：一堆紧压在一起的物料
17. It is a form of container halfway between a bale and a case：它是介于包捆和箱子之间的一种容器
18. cubic capacity：立体容积
19. facilitate handling：易于装卸

20. intended for：为……而准备
21. separate items：单个货物
22. identify goods and facilitate correct operation：识别货物及便于正确的操作
23. shipping mark, indicative mark, warning mark and supplementary mark：唛头、指示标志、警告标志和补充标志
24. FRAGILE, KEEP DRY, THIS WAY UP and CENTRE OF GRAVITY：易碎、怕湿、向上和重心点
25. Take protective measures to guarantee the good conditions of goods and the life security of people：采取保护措施来确保货物的完好无损和人们的生命安全
26. INFLAMMABLE, EXPLOSIVE, POISONOUS and RADIOACTIVE：易燃、易爆、有毒和有放射性
27. make no mentions at all：完全不提及
28. meet the special demand：满足特殊的要求

 In Practice

Questions Based on the Text

I. Decide whether the following statements are true or false according to the text.
1. One of packing's basic purposes is to protect the products. ( )
2. In transit, not all goods are necessarily packed. ( )
3. To stand long transportation of the ocean and rough handling of cargoes, the selling packing of the cargoes should be paid more attention. ( )
4. Paper, wool, cotton and carpets should be packed in drums. ( )
5. Crate is used for the lightweight goods of large cubic capacity as domestic appliance. ( )
6. Collective packing is a kind of packing whereby individual packages are put together and placed into a larger container. ( )
7. Shipping mark quickens the identification and transportation of the goods and helps avoid shipping errors. ( )
8. To ensure safe carriage of dangerous goods in transit, indicative marks are often used to indicate dangerous cargos. ( )

II. Answer these questions according to the text.
1. How do we avoid any risk of packing in international trade?

2. What is transport packing called?
3. What does common unit packing include?
4. How many parts does shipping mark consist of? What are they?
5. What is the purpose of neutral packing?

> **Business Vocabulary and Useful Expressions**

III. Translate the following terms.
1. direct steamer _____
2. promote sales _____
3. intended for _____
4. collective packing _____
5. take protective measures _____
6. safe and sound _____
7. 销售包装 _____
8. 散装货 _____
9. 唛头 _____
10. 木桶 _____
11. 有放射性的产品 _____
12. 满足特殊的要求 _____

IV. Fill in the blanks with words or phrases given below. Change the form where necessary.

| warehouse | vessel | prettify | pilferage | flexible |

1. The trucks waited at the _____ to pick up their loads.
2. The old farm workers' cottages are being _____ as holiday homes.
3. This tube is _____ but tough.
4. Besides, cartons are easy to cut open, and this increases the risk of _____.
5. It's hard to pilot a _____ in rough weather.

| conveyance | granular | halfway | explosive | supplementary |

6. The substance is hard and _____.
7. The selling party is responsible for freightage and _____ insurance.
8. There is a _____ water supply in case the main supply fails.
9. The _____ mixture in a rocket consists of both a fuel and a supply of oxygen.
10. It's about _____ between London and Bristol.

port of destination promote sales safe and sound when it comes to break down

11. No one matches him _____ swimming.
12. The rescuers brought the climbers back _____.
13. A commission on your prices would make it easier for us to _____.
14. The goods will reach the _____ on 21st, May.
15. Let's _____ the project into smaller parts in order to deal with them one by one.

➢ **Workshop**

V. Name the different ways of unit packing and give at least three examples of the goods that can be packed in this way. The first one is given:

	Unit packing: ___drum___ The related goods: 1. ___wine___ 2. _____ 3. _____
	Unit packing: _____ The related goods: 1. _____ 2. _____ 3. _____
	Unit packing: _____ The related goods: 1. _____ 2. _____ 3. _____

(Continued)

	Unit packing:＿＿＿＿＿＿＿＿
	The related goods:
	   1. ＿＿＿＿＿＿＿＿
	   2. ＿＿＿＿＿＿＿＿
	   3. ＿＿＿＿＿＿＿＿

	Unit packing:＿＿＿＿＿＿＿＿
	The related goods:
	   1. ＿＿＿＿＿＿＿＿
	   2. ＿＿＿＿＿＿＿＿
	   3. ＿＿＿＿＿＿＿＿

➤ Case Study

Suzhou WD Silk Weaving Company Limited received an inquiry from Korea AC Company, which is looking for silk scarves. After negotiating, both of them reached the agreements about the price and most of trade items. Then the importer required no marking of origin, no brand name or no WD company's name appear on the product, on the shipping packing or selling packing, on the contrary, required a specified brand designed by Korea AC Company. At the beginning, the exporter was confused by the requirement. But with the explanation of the customer, Suzhou WD Silk Weaving Company Limited signed the contract immediately.

What do we call this kind of requirement? Why did Suzhou WD Silk Weaving Company Limited sign the contract with the explanation of the customer?

Chapter 6

International Cargo Transportation and Insurance

1. Ocean Transportation

Cargo transportation is a vital link in international trade which plays apivotal role of assuring whether the buyers could receive the products timely and successfully[1].

Within all kinds of international transportation, ocean shipping (also called ocean carriage and marine transportation) accounts for the largest percentage — about 80% products are sent through ships. It means that, for example, among all the Chinese goods sold in American market, approximately, four-fifth of them have "ship tickets".

Advantages and Disadvantages of Ocean Transportation

Why do both buyer and seller all prefer to order "ship tickets" for their products? There are three main reasons. Firstly, ocean carriage is an *economical mode*[2] of transportation. Comparing to air freight, shipping freight is much lower. The second reason is its high *carrying capacity*[3] which makes shipping become one of the best choices of delivering heavy and bulky goods. The last reason is that it has less geographic constraints (most trading nations have at least one international port) than land transportation such as trains which are confined to railroads and couldn't reach to other countries overseas.

However, ocean transportation also has its weaknesses. Being *vulnerable*[4] to bad weather is the main one. Some bad weathers typhoon, rainstorm and tsunami usually cause serious effects of boat's sailing and landing, even ship sinking. Therefore, it is less *punctual*[5] by water if compared with road or air transportation. Another disadvantage is marine transportation is quite slow. Usually, the voyage from Shanghai China to West Coast of the United States takes about 15 days, and to East Coast of the United States is almost one month.

Useful Expressions and Definitions

◇ Shipping company (or called ship owner)

Usually they are *logistics companies*[6]. They own a lot of vessels and provide delivering service for exporters or importers. They help traders to transport their products to the destination by water.

◇ Booking cargo space

It is the action that trader tells ship owner that he has some goods needed to be shipped, and the amount of the products, *delivery time*[7], port of departure and destination. Then ship owner will provide shipment according to trader's acquirement. It is just like trader places an order to shipping company. Whether booking cargo space is exporter's duty or importer's depends on different payment which is negotiated between them two. For example, under FOB term, buyer has the duty to book the space, while under DES, it is seller's job.

◇ Freight forwarding

This is a company or organization which provides service for both shipping companies and traders. *Freight forwarding*[8] is like a bridge which connects those two customers. The job of freight forwarding includes: helping traders book cargo space of a shipment, preparing shipping documents, delivering products from warehouse to the port. Sometimes, traders or ship owners have their own freight forwarding departments who do all the connecting works.

Major Ocean Transpiration Modes

◇ Liner transportation

Liner transportation[9] is a vessel from one seaport to the destination port with a fixed or regular sailing route. The operation mode in a liner is similar as "a regular non-stop train" which has a comparatively fixed schedule and freight rates.

Usually if buyer and seller have a stable cooperation and regular orders, they will always tend to ship their products through liner vessel. There are two main reasons:

A. The freight rate is comparatively lower than that of other modes. Exporter could reduce the transportation expenses.

B. Because traders know shipping schedule ahead of time, may be a half year before, it is convenient for exporters to prepare the goods and have a better arrangement of their production.

◇ Freight rates

In real business, *freight rates*[10] are calculated on a weight, volume basis or product's own value. For example, some light products but with large volume, like comforters, freight rates will be charged according to the volume. On the other hand, if the products are comparatively heavy like hardware and tools, the shipping company always charges according to the weight. Freight of other products like jewelries which are small, light but expensive will refer to its value. Furthermore, there is a minimum charge of each shipping company.

There are several rules of the freight calculation:

For items marked with "W": The freight is to be calculated per metric ton on weight. It is usually called *weight ton*[11].

For items marked with "M": The freight is to be calculated per cubic meter on measurement of the cargo which is called *measurement ton*[12].

For items marked with "Ad Val": the freight is to be calculated on the basis of the price or value of the cargo.

For items marked with "W/M": the freight is to be calculated on the basis of either weight ton or measurement ton. It depends on which one is higher.

For items marked with "W/M or Ad Val": the highest rate is adopted.

There are some *surcharges*[13] in ocean transportation: in addition to the basic freight rates, there are some surcharges in shipping procedure: *bunker adjustment factor*[14], *port surcharges*[15], *transshipment surcharges*[16], *heavy lift and long length additional*[17].

◇ Tramp ships

Different from a line which has regular route and timetable, a *tramp ship*[18] is more flexible. Tramp ships don't have firm schedule and fixed route. These ships travel among many ports around the world to search and deliver cargos, especially bulks. That is to say, when a tramp ship has been landed at one port, there might be both uploading and unloading works happened at same time. Therefore, the tramp is quite like "a passenger extra" which meets peak cargo shipment demands.

◇ Charter ships

Shipping companies also offer charter services for larger orders. The trader could *charter*[19] or hire the whole vessel to carry goods. This mode is similar as "a private car" only picks up the goods belonging to the charter.

The reasons why some exporters or importers prefer chartering are that their amount of products is huge enough to fill with one boat, and also shipping company will offer special discounts to them. Therefore, the freight per ton or per cubic meter is the lowest.

Based on different pricing methods, there are two types of charter ships:

A. *Voyage charter*[20]. The fee of chartering each ship is usually based on the distance of the journal.

B. *Time charter*[21]. It is on the time basis. During the *lease term*[22], charter has the full right to use the boat. In time charter, there is another specific chartering way: the ship owner only lends the boat, while the charter hires the crew by himself. It is called *demise charter*[23].

Notes

1. Cargo transportation is a vital link in international trade which plays a pivotal role of assuring whether the buyers could receive the products timely and successfully: 货物运输是国际贸易中至关重要的一个环节,它以关键的角色保证买房是否能及时、成功地收到货物
2. economical mode: 经济的模式
3. carrying capacity: 承载量
4. vulnerable: 易受伤的
5. punctual: 准时的
6. logistics company: 物流公司
7. delivery time: 交货时间
8. freight forwarding: 货代
9. liner transportation: 班轮运输
10. freight rates: 运费费率
11. weight ton: 重量吨
12. measurement ton: 尺码吨
13. surcharges: 额外费用
14. bunker adjustment factor: 燃油附加费
15. port surcharges: 港口附加费
16. transshipment surcharges: 转船附加费
17. heavy lift and long length additional: 超重、超长附加费
18. tramp ship: 不定期货船

19. charter：租赁；承租方
20. voyage charter：程租船，根据航行距离租船
21. time charter：定期租船，根据航行时间租船
22. lease term：租期
23. demise charter：空租船，只租船不带船员的租约或租赁方

In Practice

Questions Based on the Text

I. Decide whether the following statements are true or false according to the text.

1. In international trade, most products are transported by water. (　)
2. Ocean transportation is much more expensive than air transportation. (　)
3. One of the advantages of marine transportation is punctuality. (　)
4. Freight forwarding usually has a lot of vessel and could provide shipping transportation to traders. (　)
5. Liner transportation has a fixed and regular sailing route. (　)
6. If an item is marked with "M", the freight will be calculated per cubic meter. (　)
7. If trader orders a tramp ship, there will have no crew on the boat. (　)
8. If the trader wants to rent a boat for whole year, it is better to choose voyage charter. (　)

II. Answer these questions according to the text.

1. What is ocean transportation?
2. Why ocean transportation accounts for largest transportation?
3. What are the advantages and disadvantages of ocean transportation?
4. What is the rule of calculating ocean freight?
5. What are the differences among liner transportation, tramp ships and charter ships?

Business Vocabulary and Useful Expressions

III. Translate the following terms.

1. shipping freight ＿＿＿＿＿＿
2. departure port ＿＿＿＿＿＿

3. measurement ton _____
4. booking cargo space _____
5. charter ships _____
6. shipping documents _____
7. 船运货代 _____
8. 地理环境的限制 _____
9. 船公司 _____
10. 交货时间 _____
11. 燃油附加费 _____
12. 船员 _____

IV. Fill in the blanks with words or phrases given below. Change the form where necessary.

transport   charter   punctual   bulk   flexible   depart

1. Online education gives students enough _____.
2. The train to Beijing will _____ from platform 3 in half an hour.
3. Wheat is _____ from the farms to the mills.
4. Stubbs is the soul of _____, and efficiency.
5. It is impossible to _____ a ship for the purpose.

warehouse   duty   operation   economical   constraint

6. The government imposes a special _____ on oil.
7. The country decides to reduce _____ on imports.
8. They operate three factories and a huge _____.
9. When we had done the costing on the project, it was clear it would not be _____ to go ahead with it.
10. It's too difficult for him to _____ this new sophisticated machine.

account for   confine to   compare to   are calculated on   on the basis

11. Usually the dues _____ the registered tonnage of the ship.
12. Students _____ 50% of our customers.
13. Mr. Steven is sick, so he has to _____ bed.
14. _____ of our sales forecasts, we may begin to make a profit next year.
15. _____ the city, the country looks like the world without its clothes on.

➤ Workshop

V. Look at the pictures below and choose the right rules of the freight calculation.

diamonds	1. Diamonds are probably marked with _____.
	   a. "W"
	   b. "M"
	   c. "W/M"
	   d. "Ad Val"

stuffed animals	1. Stuffed animals are probably marked with _____.
	   a. "W"
	   b. "M"
	   c. "W/M"
	   d. "Ad Val"

steel bars	1. Steel bars are probably marked with _____.
	   a. "W"
	   b. "M"
	   c. "W/M"
	   d. "Ad Val"

tires	1. Tires are probably marked with _____.
	   a. "W"
	   b. "M"
	   c. "W/M"
	   d. "Ad Val"

➢ Case Study

Officially incorporated in 2000, APL Logistics is a US $1.4 billion global supply chain services provider. APL Logistics designs and operates smart globally integrated supply chains. We combine origin and destination logistics solutions with transportation services across all modes and regions of the world.

Operating in more than 160 locations in 75 countries, we manage 200 logistics facilities covering over 20 million square feet globally. With more than 5,800 logistics professionals across the world with local market knowledge, APL logistics is your trusted global logistics partner.

If you were a manger of an export company, with you appoint APL as your shipping line?

2. Other Modes of Transportation

Apart from[1] ocean transportation, traders also prefer to choose other modes of transportation to *meet their different needs*[2], such as ocean transportation, railway transportation, road transportation and international multimodal transportation (IMT).

Air Transportation

Air transportation, the most expensive mode in international transportation, is one of the youngest forms of modern distribution. Although it *makes up a small proportion of*[3] international transportation, airplane has its own *merits*[4] and cannot be replaced.

The most obvious advantage of air freight is speed. Through air plane, goods could be delivered to any part of the world in one day without any geographical constraints. Therefore, items such as fresh fruits and flowers, seafood, *seasonal goods*[5] all tend to be delivered by plane. Other reasons that factory might choose airway are: *they want to reduce the inventory level of warehouse or delivery time is coming so that they have to transport their products as soon as possible*[6].

Another advantage is low risk of damage and high *insurance premium*[7]. So that, choosing air transportation to deliver some valuable and *fragile products*[8], like *precise* instruments[9], artworks, glassware and so on, is the best choice.

However, generally average aircraft capacity is only 2,000-25,000 kg (capacity of a shipment is usually about 50,000 ton). It leads to a high operation cost of air freight.

Railway Transportation

Railway transportation is a traditional mode of transportation which *is noted for*[10] its relatively large capacity, high speed and low cost. It is also safe, punctual and economical. Back to 1850s, gold rush *spawned*[11] the shift development of rail transportation in west American.

However, trains *are subject to*[12] iron rails which makes it is impossible, now these days, to transfer products to overseas by train. It is popular in *domestic trade*[13], business between inland countries as well as part of transportation from factory to airport and sea port.

Road Transportation

In international transportation setting, the road vehicle, same as rail transportation, is widely used for distributing goods from an inland point to the sea port or airport. Although road transportation has its limitation in capacity and vulnerable to *high risk of pilferage and damage in transit*[14], it has strength of flexibility, high distributive ability and providing door-to-door service.

International Multimodal Transportation (IMT)

Now these days, along with the rapid development of international trade, *international multimodal transportation*[15] (also called intermodal transportation) has *emerged*[16] because of variety of customers and sellers' needs, cost saving, efficiency gaining, etc. IMT this brand new mode — *just as the name implies*[17] — is to deliver products by at least two ways of transportation. For example, the products might first be delivered from factory's warehouse to sea port by truck, and then shipped to destination port, last, transported to buyer's warehouse by train.

In the real business, no matter how many modes are used in one trade, only one transportation operator takes the whole responsibility of distribution from taking the cargo from the *consignor*[18] to delivering them to the *consignee*[19]. Therefore, only one carriage contract is signed between consignor and logistics and one freight rate for the whole journey are applicable to the whole journey.

Usually, in intermodal transportation, it is more convenient to put goods in *containers*[20] which reduce the work amount of *cargo handling*[21]. Hence, this method could maintain security, reduce the losses and the damages, and make faster delivery.

◇ Useful expressions for container service

FCL (Full Container Load)[22]: It means the whole container load, or the load that reaches its allowable maximum (or full) weight or measurement.

LCL (Less than Container Load)[23]: It means the container is not full. Those products are called *loose cargo*[24].

CFS (Container Freight Station)[25]: *It is the place where carrier receives all the LCL for containerization*[26]. Usually those stations are Logistics Company's or freight forwarding's warehouse.

CY (container yard)[27]: It is the location where all the FCL is delivered. Usually it is near sea port or air port.

Modes of container service

There are four main modes in container service: CY/CY, CY/CFS, CFS/CY and CFS/CFS.

CY/CY (house to house or door to door): This service starts from carrier sending containers to consigner's warehouse for loading goods to carrier transporting those containers to consignee's warehouse. Usually this service is suit for FCL.

CY/CFS (door to CFS): This service starts from carrier sending containers to consigner's warehouse for *loading goods*[28] to carrier transporting those containers to container freight station close to the port of destination. Therefore, buyers should pick up good from station by themselves.

CFS/CY (CFS to door): Consigner sends goods to CFS. Then carrier delivers products to buyer's warehouse.

CFS/CFS: Consigner sends goods to CFS. Then carrier delivers products to container freight station close to the port destination. Buyers should pick up goods from station by themselves.

Those four services are generally adopted in different occasions:

CY/CY: Buyer orders whole containers from one seller.

CY/CFS: Seller exports products in a container to more than one receiver.

CFS/CY: Buyer receives products in a container from more than one sender.

CFS/CFS: This is usually for loose cargo.

 Notes

1. apart from：除了
2. meet their different needs：满足不同的需求
3. make up a small proportion of：所占比例很小
4. merit：长处
5. seasonal goods：季节性货物
6. They want to reduce the inventory level of warehouse or delivery time is coming so that they have to transport their products as soon as possible：由于(卖方)要减少库存(降低仓库运营成本)或交货日期临近(预期买家未收到货物,卖方须支付赔偿款),他们必须尽快运走货物。
7. insurance premium：保险赔偿款
8. fragile product：易碎货物
9. precise instrument：精密仪器
10. be noted for：以……著名
11. spawn：产生
12. are subject to：受限于
13. domestic trade：国内贸易
14. high risk of pilferage and damage in transit：(货物)在运送过程中易被盗和损坏
15. international multimodal transportation：国际多式联运
16. emerge：出现
17. just as the name implies：顾名思义
18. consignor：发货人
19. consignee：收货人
20. container：集装箱
21. cargo handling：货物装卸
22. FCL (Full Container Load)：集装箱整箱
23. LCL (Less than Container Load)：集装箱拼箱
24. loose cargo：散货,装不满一整个集装箱的货
25. CFS (Container Freight Station)：集装箱营运站
26. It is the place where carrier receives all the LCL for containerization：它(集装箱营运站)是接受拼箱货物并装成整箱的地方
27. CY (container yard)：集装箱堆场,堆放集装箱的地方,通常也是货运公司装卸集装箱

的地方
28. load goods：装卸货物

In Practice

➤ Questions Based on the Text

I. Decide whether the following statements are true or false according to the text.
1. Buyer who sells fresh sea shrimps and fish probably chooses air transportation.　　　　　　　　　　　　　　　　　　　　　　　（　）
2. Air transportation has low insurance premium.　　　　　　　（　）
3. The capacity of air transportation is very small.　　　　　　（　）
4. Through rail transportation, cargo could be delivered to overseas.（　）
5. Trucks have high risks in transportation.　　　　　　　　　（　）
6. International multimodal transportation means to deliver products by at least two ways of transportation.　　　　　　　　　　　　　（　）
7. In one IMT, consignor could hire more than one carrier to deliver the cargo.　　　　　　　　　　　　　　　　　　　　　　　　（　）
8. If the amount of cargo is small and couldn't fill one container, the best choice is to use CY/CY service.　　　　　　　　　　　　　　（　）

II. Answer these questions according to the text.
1. In what occasions, consignor prefers to use air transportation?
2. What are the demerits of air transportation?
3. Why the proportions of those three transportations (air, rail, and road) are lower than that of ocean transportation?
4. Why IMT is so popular now and what are its advantages?
5. How should consignor select container service?

➤ Business Vocabulary and Useful Expressions

III. Translate the following terms.
1. modern distribution _____
2. reduce the inventory level of warehouse _____

3. insurance premium _____
4. pilferage and damage _____
5. distributive ability _____
6. consignee _____
7. 装卸货物 _____
8. 季节性货物 _____
9. 易碎物品 _____
10. 空运载重 _____
11. 淘金热 _____
12. 门到门服务 _____

IV. Fill in the blanks with words or phrases given below. Change the form where necessary.

| proportion | merit | replace | obvious | inventory |

1. The embassy is an _____ target for terrorist attacks.
2. A large _____ of my time is spent in studying.
3. The _____ showed that the store was overstocked.
4. Charms strikes the sight, but _____ wins the soul.
5. We've _____ the old adding machine with a computer.

| insurance | precise | spawn | domestic | containerization |

6. His _____ is $300 a year.
7. The fish were madly pushing their way upstream to _____.
8. With the new technique, measurement was claimed to be much more _____.
9. Think that _____ is one of the best transportation methods at present.
10. We adopt an active attitude towards drawing on overseas fund to make up for _____ fund shortage.

| apart from | are subject to | is noted for | just as | no matter how |

11. Every substance in the world, _____ different it may seem from any other substance, is made partly of electrons.
12. It was _____ I had conjectured.
13. _____ the injuries to his face and hands, he broke both legs.
14. Quantity and price stated in the invoice _____ our final confirmation.
15. The west lake _____ its scenery.

Chapter 6
International Cargo Transportation and Insurance

> ## Workshop

V. Look at the flow chart below and discuss the transportation procedure.

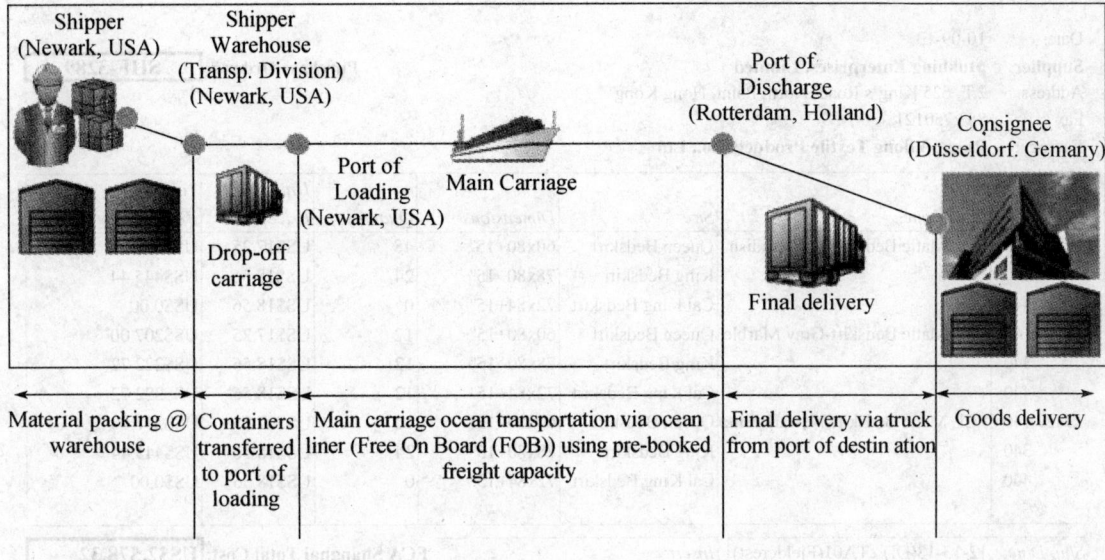

> ## Case Study

Shanghai remained the world's busiest container port in 2013 as the city moved toward its goal of becoming a shipping center.

Container through put rose 3.3 percent to a record 33.6 million TEUs (Twenty-foot Equivalent Units) last year, official data showed yesterday. The city first became the world's biggest container port in 2010 when it surpassed Singapore.

Could you search more information about the achievement in Shanghai shipping?

3. Shipment Clause, Bill of Lading

Shipment Clause

Before buyer and seller sign an international trading contract and place an order, some important *shipment clauses*[1] should be negotiated which usually cover *time of shipment and* delivery[2]; port (place) of shipment and destination[3]; partial shipment and transshipment[4]. Those clauses are identified detailedly in purchasing orders (Figure 6-3-1).

Sunham Home Fashions
136 Madison Avenue 16th Floor · New York, NY 10016
Phone: 212 695 1218 · Fax: 212 947 4793

Date: 10-09-13
Supplier: Mokhing Enterprises, Limited   Purchase Order #: **SHF-3289**
Address: 2/F, 625 King's Road, North Point, Hong Kong
Fax #: 853 750121
Factory: Rugao Yilong Textile Products Co., Ltd

Item #	Item Name	Size	Dimensions	Quantity	Unit Price	Total Price
13828 140	FCL Matte Bedskirt-Horseradish	Queen Bedskirt	60x80+15"	48	US$17.25	US$828.00
340		King Bedskirt	78x80+15"	24	US$18.56	US$445.44
440		Cal King Bedskirt	72x84+15"	0	US$18.56	US$0.00
13826 140	FCL Matte Bedskirt-Gray Marble	Queen Bedskirt	60x80+15"	12	US$17.25	US$207.00
340		King Bedskirt	78x80+15"	12	US$18.56	US$222.72
440		Cal King Bedskirt	72x84+15"	12	US$18.56	US$222.72
13827 140	FCL Matte Bedskirt-Newark Blue	Queen Bedskirt	60x80+15"	12	US$17.25	US$207.00
340		King Bedskirt	78x80+15"	24	US$18.56	US$445.44
440		Cal King Bedskirt	72x84+15"	0	US$18.56	US$0.00

Ship Date: 12-13-13(DI) TA01(Fieldcrest)   Insert: FCA Shanghai Total Cost: **US$2,578.32**
Terms: T/T 80   FCL
Ship To: Shanghai, PRC

Special Instructions:
Description: 100% Cotton Drop Bedskirt;
Exchange Rate: 6.8766:1
Case Pack: 3-3-3
Customer PO#: 5872472
Please deliver original documen to Sunham Shanghai Office.

Comments:
1 Supplier must pack with inserts and UPC labels.
2 Supplier must mark all cartons with Sunham, PO #, Item #, Size, and Quantity.
3 Care labels must have Sunham RN # 82817, care instructions and fabric content.
4 Law labels must have Reg. No. PA-24262 (RC), sizes, fabric content and country of origin.
5 Supplier must submit a complete set of original documents including B/L, visa, invoice, and packing list to our designated bank or directly to Sunham within one week of shipment.
6 Supplier must fax copies of all documents to Sunham immediately upon shipment.
7 Title and risk of loss to be transferred from Mokhing to Sunham at the International Date Line

Bank Address:
Hong Kong Bank
452 5th Ave, 14th Floor
New York, NY 10018 USA
Attention:
HSBC Trade Services
K.P. Choi or Vicky Chan

Buyer's Signature   Seller's Signature

Figure 6-3-1 purchasing order

◇ Time of shipment and time of delivery

Time of shipment means the departure time of the ship which carries the cargo from departure port to destination port, while time of delivery is the *due day*[5] that seller hands over the products at the agreed place and finishes his tasks.

For all *shipment contracts*[6], such as FOB, CFR, CIF, FCA, CFT and CIP, those two can be used *interchangeably*[7] in the contract. In FOB contract, for example, seller has the duty to deliver the products from his warehouse to port, so time of shipment in this contract is the same as time of delivery. Seller has to deliver the products to ship before due day.

On the other hand, in all arrival contracts, for example, DAF, DES, DEQ, DDU and DDP, the seller has responsibility for all risks of bringing the goods to the named destination. Therefore, delivery time is usually when the customer receives the cargo. Then, time of shipment should be a couple of days or weeks before delivery according to the time for the journey. The seller has to arrange shipment *cautiously*[8] and could deliver the products a little bit earlier in order to avoid penalty for late delivery because of any delaying during the journey.

Time of shipment or delivery is a very important clause in contract as it *stipulates*[9] the due time and declares *violation*[10] of contract if there is any delay or advance of delivery. Normally, there are two types of describing time clause:

1. Clearly specifying a period of time or a deadline:
   Shipment during May 2014;
   Shipment not later than 15th July, 2014.
2. Setting a time period upon receipt of payment:
   Shipment within 30 days after receipt of L/C.

Cautions, avoid using *ambiguous phrases*[11] as "immediate shipment", "shipment as soon as possible". Such imprecise time likely causes dispute whether cargos are delayed or not.

◇ Port of shipment and destination

Port of shipment means which port the goods are shipped and depart from while port of destination is the port where cargos are ultimately discharged. Both of them should be clearly specified in the contract.

There are hundreds of international ports along coastline. Some of them which have deepwater harbor, huge throughput and enormous influence in international trade are called International Shipping Center such as London, New York, Rotterdam, Shanghai, Hong Kong, Singapore, etc. Those centers have three main operation modes:

1. Shipping centers, like London, mainly provide shipping affairs operation and shipping service. Those centers are usually traditional international ports full of trading and sailing culture. Although the throughput is not as enormous as other's now these days, they are famous of providing *chartering vessel*[12], *financing of shipbuilding industry*[13], vessel

insurance and other services.

2. Shipping centers, like Hong Kong and Singapore, are usually *transshipment station*[14]. Those ports usually have small *economic hinterland*[15] with less own cargo resources, but located in many important sailing courses. Benefiting from their free trade policy, those ports are popular of *entrepot trade*[16] and transshipment.

3. The third mode provides cargo distribution service for hinterland, such as Shanghai, New York and Rotterdam. Those ports are located in big countries with huge product exportation and importation.

◇ Partial shipment and transshipment

Partial shipment means *goods in one contract are to be shipped in lots*[17]. Due to large quantity of the transaction or the limitation of supplies and transportation, sometimes in international trade, traders have to choose partial shipment. However, if contract doesn't state products are shipped partially, all the cargos need to be delivered at the same time from one boat.

Transshipment means reloading and transferring during the course of carriage from the port of loading to the port of discharge. For example, some exporting shipment from China might transship at Hong Kong which is a famous transshipment shipping center. The reasons for adopting transshipment may include one or more of the following: few or no available ships sailing directly to the port of destination; no suitable ships are available at the stipulated period; freight of transshipment might be lower than direct shipment; the amount of cargo for a certain port of destination is so small that no tramp ships will call at that port. Same as partial shipment, if no such clause is stated in the contract, transshipment *are construed as*[18] not allowed.

Bill of Lading

The most important transportation document, the *bill of lading*[19] is issued by carrier to shipper after shipment. Usually, after freight forwarding or shipping company receives the cargo, they will send shipper a sample B/L for confirming. Shipper has to check all the information on the B/L are correct, including amount, item name, ship date, and departure and destination port. Any small mistakes will cause difficulties of receiving products and any revision of original B/L causes extra fee from shipping company. After shipper confirms it is all correct, the full set of original bill of landing will be released from shipping company after shipment date. (Figure 6-3-2)

BILL OF LADING

Shipper: KOESTER GMBH & CO. KG INDUSTRIESTRASSE 2 96146 ALTENDORF GERMANY	Shipper's Ref. AU018185 Country of Origin	Bill of Lading No. NUEWUHA00176 Shipment No. 9/1202/003649
Consignee (if "To Order" so indicate) L+L HEALTHCARE HUBEI CO. LTD. HONGSHAN INDUSTRIAL PARK QUINGQUAN TOWN 434025 438200 XISHUI COUNTY, HUBEI PROVINCE CHINA		PELORUS OCEAN LINE LIMITED Room 905, Silvercord Tower II, 30 Canton Road, Tsimshatsui, Kowloon / Hong Kong
Notify Party (No claim shall attach for failure to notify) SAME AS CONSIGNEE	For Delivery Please Apply To HELLMANN WORLDWIDE LOGISTICS ROOM 1211, BLK 1, ATTN.: MS. WANG YOU HONG NEW WORLD INT'L TRADING TOWER 568 JIANSHE AVENUE, Tel: +86 27 8555 0522 / Fax: +86 27 8555 0722	
	Port of Transhipment (if applicable)	Transhipment Vessel (if applicable)

Pre-Carriage by	Place of Receipt BREMEN CFS	Port of Loading HAMBURG	
Vessel APL FINLAND / MOL8629	Port of Discharge WUHAN VIA HONG KONG	Place of Delivery WUHAN CFS	No. of Original Bills of Lading 3 / THREE

Marks & Numbers	Number of pkgs. or shipping units	Description of Goods and Pkgs.	Gross Weight	Measurement
FCL/LCL CONTAINER NO/SEAL NO TCIU8739743/KL1531494/PART OF 40'HC/6PA/2831,000KG/5,707CBM/(FCL/FCL)				
AU018185/1-6	6 PALLETS	ADHESIVE TAPE	2831,000 KG	5,707 CBM
L+L HEALTHCARE HUBEI CO. LTD. HONGSHAN INDUSTRIAL PARK QUINGQUAN TOWN 434025 XISHUI COUNTY HUBEI PROVINCE, PRC (438200)				
	6 PALLETS ==========			
TOTAL: SIX (6) PALLETS ONLY			2831,000 KG //FREIGHT PREPAID//	5,707 CBM

	Total No of Pkgs. 6	Temperature Control Instructions:	COPY NON-NEGOTIABLE
Freight Payable At HAMBURG			Excess Value Declaration: Refer to Clause 6 (3) (B) + (C) on reverse side
Freight Details, Charges Etc.			Special Clauses

RECEIVED by the Carrier the Goods as specified above in apparent good order and condition unless otherwise stated, to be transported to such place as agreed, authorized or permitted herein and subject to all terms & conditions appearing on the front and reverse of this Bill of Lading to which the Merchant agrees by accepting this Bill of Lading, any local privileges and customs notwithstanding.

The particulars given above as stated by the shipper and the weight, measure, quantity, condition, contents and value of the Goods are unknown to the Carrier.

One of the original bills of lading shall be presented to the Carrier or his agent, duly endorsed, before cargo shall be released, and the other(s) to become void.

Shipped On Board The Vessel		Place and Date of Issue HAMBURG, 12.04.2010
HAMBURG	On (date) 12.04.2010	Signed on behalf of the Carrier: PELORUS OCEAN LINE
Signed By HELLMANN WORLDWIDE LOGISTICS GMBH & CO. KG		HELLMANN WORLDWIDE LOGISTICS GMBH & CO. KG By: _____
As Agents for Carrier Pelorus Ocean Line		As Agents

Figure 6-3-2 bill of landing

Bill of lading has a lot of functions in transportation.

◇ A receipt of cargo

B/L acts as a receipt for the goods received. It states the conditions in which the goods are delivered to the carrier and shipped successfully.

◇ Evidence of the contract of carriage.

Bill of lading is a typical type of contract between carrier and shipper which states the legal cooperation of transportation. Hens, carrier has the duty to deliver the cargos to destination safely.

◇ Document of title to the goods.

The person who produces a bill of lading owns the cargo and has the right to pick up the goods from carrier. In international trade, shippers if they are sellers, have to send original B/L to buyers for them to receive the cargo.

 Notes

1. shipment clause：装运条款
2. time of shipment and delivery：船期与交货时间
3. port of shipment and destination：出发港和目的港
4. partial shipment and transshipment：分批装运和转运
5. due day：到期日
6. shipment contract：船运合同
7. interchangeably：可交换地
8. cautiously：谨慎地
9. stipulate：规定；保证
10. violation：违背；妨碍
11. ambiguous phrase：模凌两可的条款
12. chartering vessel：租船
13. financing of shipbuilding industry：为造船业融资
14. transshipment station：转运站
15. economic hinterland：经济腹地

16. entrepot trade：转口贸易
17. goods in one contract are to be shipped in lots：一份合同内的货物分几批发货
18. are construed as：解释为
19. bill of lading：提单

 In Practice

➤ Questions Based on the Text

I. Decide whether the following statements are true or false according to the text.

1. In all the cases, time of delivery means the exact time of the shipment. (   )
2. In DAF and DEQ contracts, the seller has responsibility for all risks of bringing the goods to the named destination. (   )
3. Port of shipment means which port the goods are shipped and depart from. (   )
4. Hong Kong and Singapore are famous of providing chartering vessel, financing of shipbuilding industry, vessel insurance and other services. (   )
5. Partial shipment means reloading and transferring during the course of carriage from the port of loading to the port of discharge. (   )
6. If there is few or no available ships sailing directly to the port of destination, seller could choose transshipment. (   )
7. After the two parties sign the contract, buyer can receive the bill of lading immediately. (   )
8. The person who owns the B/L has the right to pick up the goods from carrier. (   )

II. Answer these questions according to the text.

1. What is shipment clause?
2. What is the difference between time of shipment and time of delivery?
3. When sellers will choose partial shipment and when they will choose transshipment?
4. What is London shipping center famous of?
5. When the buyer can receive the bill of lading?

➤ Business Vocabulary and Useful Expressions

III. Translate the following terms.

1. transshipment _____

2. partial shipment _____
3. financing of shipbuilding industry _____
4. due day _____
5. shipment contract _____
6. shipment clause _____
7. 谨慎地安排船期 _____
8. 违约 _____
9. 超出交货日期 _____
10. 模凌两可的条款 _____
11. 货运中心 _____
12. 经济腹地 _____

IV. Choose the right words to describe the shipping centers.

Shipping Center	Description
London	
Singapore	
Shanghai	
Hong Kong	
Rotterdam	
New York	

> Workshop

V. Look at those two pictures, and discuss the reasons behind the pictures. If you are the carrier or the cargo owner, what will inspire you?

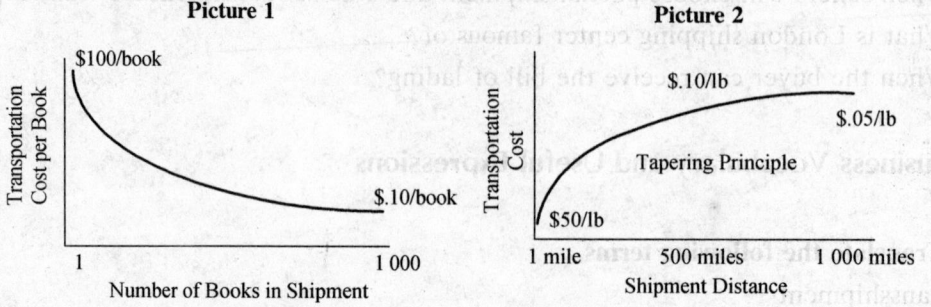

Picture 1   Picture 2

> **Case Study**

ABC Company signed a large export contract stipulating, "Shipment will be made during August of 2013". But due to the problems with the vessel, seller could not book a shipment until September 13.

What could be the consequence of shipment delay? What should the carrier do in order to avoid shipment delay?

4. International Cargo Transportation Insurance

Risk is a common word and also one of the last words we want to hear in our daily life. People might suffer the lost of relatives' or friends life, their own property or the pain of the illness and high medical expenses. Hence, many insurance agents *are designed to*[1] providing insurance service which could make *financial compensation*[2] to victims.

During the cargo transportation, risk exists at each stage of journey in all kinds of cargo delivery. They may face all kinds of losses and damage. It is important and essential for cargo owners to insure the products.

Useful Expressions of All Parties

Insurer[3]: It could also be called "*underwriter*[4]". Insurer usually refers to the insurance company or the individual who runs an insurance firm. Insurer receives the *insurance premium*[5] and promise to *indemnify*[6] losses or damages according to the insurance contract.

Insured[2]: Insured indicates the individual or organization who buys insurance from the insurer. They are the person who pay insurance premium. It could also be called "policyholder" or "insurance applicant".

Claimant[8]: Claimant is same as *beneficiary*[9] who acclaims the lost and receives the financial compensation from insurer when there are losses or damages of cargo during transportation.

Insurance broker[10]: (It also insurance agent) sells, solicits, or negotiates insurance for compensation.

Four Fundament Principles of Cargo Insurance

Insurance Law of the People's Republic of China which issued in 1995 defines four basics principles. They are *insurable interest principle*[11], *the utmost good faith principle*[12], *the indemnity principle*[13] *and the proximate cause principle*[14].

◇ Insurable interest principle

Insurable interest principle means the right of accepting the financial or other kind of benefit from the insured objects. In international trade when there is cargos loss of or damage to, the insured has an insurable interest.

◇ The utmost good faith principle

Both insurer and insured should keep their word according to the insurance contract. The insurance clauses are detailed and clarified in the contract by insurer. On the other hand, insured reports the losses and damages authentically and validly. However, in order to avoid the chances of *false claim*[15] and ambiguous insurance clauses, basically, both parties prefer to rely upon the third party — the proposer or the broker acting as an *arbitration*[16] and *intendance*[17].

◇ The indemnity principle

Indemnity principle *prescribes*[18] that the insured should not profit from a loss or damage but should be returned (as near as possible) to the same financial position that existed before the loss or damage occurred. In other words, the insured cannot recover more than his or her actual loss from the insurer. However, there are certain exceptions to this rule, such as personal accident and life insurance policies where the policy amount is paid on occurrence of accident or death and the question of profit does not arise. Some marine insurance policies also constitute an exception because the settlement of a total loss is based on a sum agreed upon at the time the insurance policy was written.

◇ The proximate cause principle

During the international delivery, there are many causes that leads to the loss of or damage to the goods insured. The proximate cause principle, or to be called direct-cause principle, is therefore employed in the judgment of causation between accidents and losses. The insurer only has liability to pay compensation for the loss which is only from a peril insured against has occurred. It means that the insurer shall only be responsible for the loss which has a direct link to the risks covered.

Notes

1. be designed to：适用于
2. financial compensation：经济赔偿
3. insurer：保险公司；承保方
4. underwriter：保险公司；承保方
5. insurance premium：保险费
6. indemnify：保证；赔偿；保险
7. insured：保险购买人
8. claimant：受益方，索赔方
9. beneficiary：受益方，索赔方
10. insurance broker：保险代理人
11. insurable interest principle：保险利益原则
12. the utmost good faith principle：最大诚信原则
13. the indemnity principle：补偿原则
14. the proximate cause principle：近因原则
15. false claim：谎报
16. arbitration：仲裁；公断
17. intendance：监督；管理；行政管理部门
18. prescribe：规定

In Practice

> ### Questions Based on the Text

I. Decide whether the following statements are true or false according to the text.
   1. Usually, money is a commonly method of compensation to victims.   (   )
   2. Now these days, transportation is quite safe, so most of seller won't insure the cargo.   (   )
   3. Claimant is the individual or organization who runs an insurance firm.   (   )
   4. Another word for insurance broker is insurance agent.   (   )
   5. Insurable interest principle means the right of accepting the financial or other kind

of benefit from the insured objects.

6. The function of insurance broker which acts as an arbitration and intendance is to ensure utmost good faith. ( )
7. Based on indemnity principle, the insured cannot gain more money than his or her actual loss from the insurer. ( )
8. Direct-cause principle means the insurer is only responsible for the loss which has a direct link to the risks covered. ( )

II. Answer these questions according to the text.
1. Why international cargo transportation insurance is so important?
2. Usually who is the insured?
3. If there is a damage of the cargo, who will receive the financial compensation?
4. What are the four insurance principles guiding insurance practice?
5. Which party ensure fair and just in compensation?

> Business Vocabulary and Useful Expressions

III. Translate the following terms.
1. financial compensation _____
2. underwriter _____
3. insurance premium _____
4. insurance broker _____
5. the proximate cause principle _____
6. insurable interest principle _____
7. 风险 _____
8. 受益人 _____
9. 谎报 _____
10. 仲裁 _____
11. 保险合同 _____
12. 保险条款 _____

> Workshop

IV. Look at the statements below and choose the right answer.
A. The person or organization offers insurance policies in return for premiums.
B. A person who contracts for an insurance policy that indemnifies him against loss

of property or life or health etc.

C. An agent who sells insurance.

D. A person who can get financial compensation if his or her interests are damaged or lost.

E. A person whose interests are protected by an insurance policy.

F. A financial institution that sells insurance.

1. insurer _____
2. insured _____
3. claimant _____
4. insurance broker _____

> **Case Study**

An importer signed an FOB contract with an Italian company, importing a batch of leather shoes. The contract required that goods be carried by containers. The goods were packed as follows: each pair of shoes in a plastic bag, four sets of shoes to a large polyethylene bag. The importer effected insurance against WPA and War Risks. When goods arrived at the destination, the goods were found wet to different extents. Upon careful investigation, finally the importer found that there were several holes on the top of the container, the biggest of which was as big as 4 cm in diameter. The importer faxed the exporter, asking for compensation. However, the exporter suggested the importer should lodge a claim against the insurer for compensation.

Please comment on this case and work out the solution.

Chapter 7

International payment

1. Paying Instrument

No matter what kind of products is sold and what type of transportation is used through international trading, the ultimate objective of purchasing and selling is the exchange of money and products. Therefore paying is an *inevitable procedure*[1] and also one of the most important steps.

During paying procedure, because of the large sum of price and long distance between two parties, it is almost impossible that buyers directly pay sellers with cash. *Ready money business*[2] seldom appears in international trading. Therefore, *instead of cash, they need some documents which have legal authority for exchange*[3]. Those documents which are called paying instrument are the evidence of a *financial transaction*[4]. They have the same power and value of cash. Some examples of instruments are *bills of exchange*[5], *checks*[6], *promissory notes*[7] and so on.

Bill of Exchange

Bills of exchange are financial documents that require the individual or business that is addressed in the document to pay a specified amount of money on a date that is cited within the text. *They can be drawn by individuals or banks and are generally transferable by*[8] *endorsements*[9]. This type of document will also *require the authorized signature of the debtor in order to be considered legal and binding*[10].

In bills of exchange, there are three parties: the drawer, the drawee and the payee.

Drawer: The drawer is the one who draws or issues the bill. After seller receives the cargo they authorizes bank to write a bill of exchange to demand drawee to pay a certain sum of money to the payee.

Drawee: The drawee is the one who needs to pay the money to the payee. (If it is a

Banker's bills of exchange, drawer is also the bank.)

Payee: The payee of the bill of exchange is the creditor of the bill of exchange. He has the right to ask the drawee for the payment.

A bill of exchange is also called a draft which is one of the *credit instruments*[11] in international trade. The typical bill of exchange has the following items (Figure 7-1-1):

The words of "Bill of Exchange" or "Draft".

The date and place of issuance of the draft.

A specific sum which shall be exactly the same as that indicated on export invoice.

The period of credit, or called tenor.

The name of the drawee.

The name and signature of the drawer.

The name of the payee or order or bearer.

The endorsement of the payee when applicable.

Figur 7-1-1 bill of exchange

◇ Types of bill of exchange

(1) Commercial draft and banker's draft. According to different drawee, there are two types of draft. A commercial draft is normally issued by a firm on another firm or a bank. *If the drawee is the bank, the B/E is a banker's draft which is a secure payment and the most widely used type*[12]. Before importer's bank pays the money to payee, the bank needs to collect certain amount of security money from buyer according to buyer's degrees of comparison. After payment, the bank has debtor-creditor relationship with buyer.

(2) Clean bill and documentary bill. When a clean bill is issued, other commercial

documents needn't to be enclosed. On the other hand, a documentary bill does have the attachments of relevant commercials documents, especially the transportation documents evidencing the title to cargoes.

(3) Sight draft and time draft. On the draft, the time when payee receives the money is clarified. It defines whether seller could get money immediately or after a period of time. Sight draft means payment will be made when shipment reaches its destination. On a sight draft, there are the words as "at sight of this bill of exchange, pay to ..." A time draft is used when the exporter extends a certain period of credit to the buyer. Normally, the words that appear on draft are "at 30/60/90 days sight of this bill of exchange, pay to ..."

Promissory Note

Promissory note (Figure 7-1-2) is a written instrument which contains an unconditional promise whereby the maker undertakes to pay a definite sum of money to the payee or to his order. It is a *negotiable instrument*[13] which right could be transferred to another receiver under certain situation. Promissory note which is issued by bank is the widely used type because it is the most secured paying instrument. That means before the buyer applies the bank to issue a promissory note, buyer has to have the same amount of money in his account. Different from bill of exchange, the bank has no debtor-creditor relationship with note maker. There are only two parties in promissory note — maker and payee.

Promissory note

For value received, the undersigned promises to pay to the order of BancZone, Inc.

the sum of: _____*****Ten-Thousand and no/100 Dollars*****_____

Along with annual interest of 8% on the unpaid balance. This note shall mature and be payable, along with accrued interest, on June 30, 20X8.

____*January 1, 20X8*____ ____*Oliva Zavala*____
Issue Date Maker signature

Figure 7-1-2 promissory note

Check

A check (Figure 7-1-3) is an unconditional order signed by the drawer, requiring the banker to pay on demand a certain sum of money to the order of a specified person or to *bearer*[14]. Along with the development of convenient transferring accounts through internet and widely using of credit card, using check these days is not as popular as last century. Because most cheeks are hand written, it is not as secured as promissory note and bill of exchange as well. However, it is still an important type of paying instrument.

When drawer issues the check, he must be sure that the amount carried on the check is not more than the *balance amount*[15] he has deposited in the bank, or *the check will be dishonored*[16]. On the other hand, when the exporter has received check from the importer for the payment, it is better for him to come to the paying bank first to see if it can be cashed. If there is no problem of the check, the payee could receive the money within one or two days.

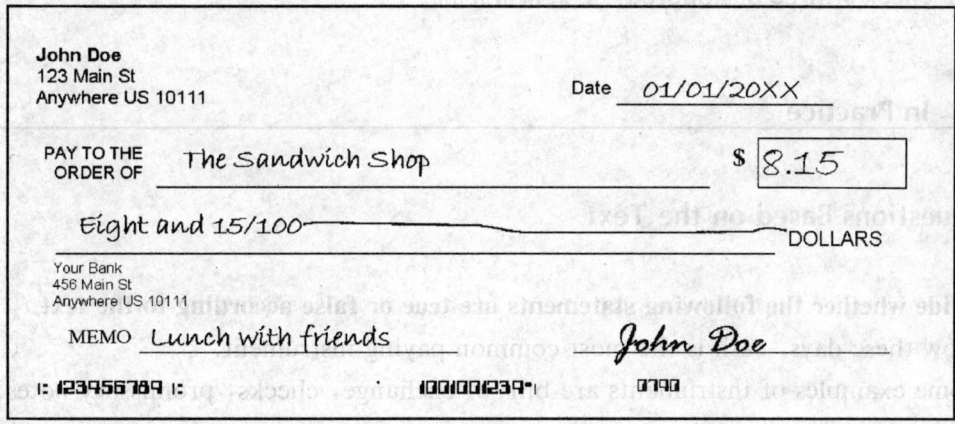

Figure 7-1-3 check

 Notes

1. inevitable procedure: 不可避免的步骤
2. ready money business: 现金交易
3. Instead of cash, they need some documents which have legal authority for exchange: 购买双方需要一些有法律效用的文件来代替现金作为交换凭证
4. financial transaction: 经济交易
5. bill of exchange: 汇票
6. check: 支票

7. promissory note：本票
8. They can be drawn by individuals or banks and are generally transferable by endorsements：他们(汇票)可以由个人或银行签发,并通常可通过背书来转让
9. endorsement：支持；背书
10. require the authorized signature of the debtor in order to be considered legal and binding：为了保证合法和有法律效力,需要债务人的签名授权
11. credit instrument：借据,有信用保障的凭证
12. If the drawee is the bank, the B/E is a banker's draft which is a secure payment and the most widely used type：如果付款人是银行,那这样的汇票是银行汇票。这种汇票比较安全,且运用范围广
13. negotiable instrument：可转让票据
14. bearer：持票者
15. the balance amount：账户余额
16. the check will be dishonored：支票将被拒付

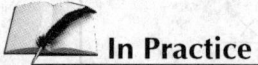

In Practice

➤ Questions Based on the Text

I. Decide whether the following statements are true or false according to the text.

1. Now these days, cash is the most common paying instrument. （   ）
2. Some examples of instruments are bills of exchange, checks, promissory notes. （   ）
3. Bill of exchange can be drawn by individuals or banks and are generally transferable by endorsements. （   ）
4. In bill of exchange, the drawer is the one who needs to pay the money to the payee. （   ）
5. If the drawee is the bank, the B/E is secured by bank and the most widely used type. （   ）
6. Promissory note is a written instrument which contains a conditional promise. （   ）
7. If the bank has no debtor-creditor relationship with note maker, the instrument is promissory note. （   ）
8. If the drawer has no amount in his bank account, the check he issues will not be dishonored. （   ）

Chapter 7
International Payment

II. Answer these questions according to the text.
1. Why international traders prefer to use paying instrument?
2. What are the three types of paying instrument which are widely used now?
3. Among of all the types of bill of exchange, which one is the most secured?
4. What are the differences between bill of exchange and promissory note?
5. What's the disadvantage and advantage of check?

➢ **Business Vocabulary and Useful Expressions**

III. Translate the following terms.
1. inevitable procedure _____
2. ready money business _____
3. endorsement _____
4. authorized signature _____
5. credit instrument _____
6. documentary bill _____
7. 经济交易 _____
8. 汇票 _____
9. 本票 _____
10. 支票 _____
11. 可转让票据 _____
12. 持票者 _____

IV. Fill in the blanks with words or phrases given below. Change the form where necessary.

| inevitable authority transaction endorsement credit |

1. They are working hard for the _____ of China.
2. For the first time he realized the pain _____ in any human relationship.
3. Both the _____ and the media wondered whether insider dealing had been going on.
4. These measures have the strong _____ of the Labor party.
5. Had you not helped us, we should have canceled this _____.

| documentary attachment promissory negotiable secure |

6. When one borrows from a bank, one signs a _____ note.
7. The _____ is combined with the contract.

147

8. If you are not sure it is _____, do not debug it.
9. This great battle was vividly recorded in the _____ film.
10. Payment may be made by way of letters of credit or _____ instruments.

➢ Workshop

V. Checks, bills and notes often contain sums of money in two forms: figures and words. Please spell out the following figures.

1. US $ 897,343 _____
2. £ 100,000,000 _____
3. ¥ 1,878,333,000 _____
4. JPY23,330,000 _____
5. €12,000 _____

➢ Case Study

Read the bill of exchange below and answer the questions.

```
                                                    TWO COPIES
No. 80W5069-2              Date: 4th DEC. 2008
EXCHANGE FOR   USD63,162.00
At 90 DAYS sight of this FIRST OF EXCHANGE (second of the same tenor and date
unpaid) pay to the order of OURSELVES the sum of _____ Value received
Draw under LC No. 314955B OF IST AUG. 1999 ISSUED BY YOURGOODSEL VES
TO HORNER              HENAN NATIVE PRODUCE & ANIMAL
TRUST CO.              BY-PRODUCTS IMP. & EXP. CO.
PITTSBURG                        _____
                                  MANAGER
```

1. Who is the drawer/drawee?
2. On which day was the draft drawn?
3. Is the bill in sola (one copy) or two?
4. How much money is involved?
5. How long is this bill valid?
6. According to the bill, what is the mode of payment used?

Chapter 7
International Payment

2. Payment Methods

When the two parties — exporter and importer — negotiate the details of contract and order, they have to make the agreement of which method of payment will be conducted. *Payment methods, that are different from paying instruments which are financial documents, are a series of activities or operations facilitating the movement of funds from one party to the other*[1]. There are three main types of method: *remittance*[2], *collection*[3] and *letter of credit*[4].

Procedure and Related Parties of Remittance

Remittance is also called *favorable exchange*[5] which is the simplest one among the three methods of payment and also the most widely used method under international trading setting. Four parties are involved in remittance: the remitter (importer, payer), the payee or beneficiary (exporter, payee), the remitting bank (importer's bank) and the paying bank (exporter's bank). After the business transaction finishes, the remitter (importer) instructs his remitting bank to "remit" or send the transaction amount to the beneficiary (exporter).

Among those four parties, the detailed procedure of remittance is as illustrated.

◇ The remitter, who is the importer, submits a remittance application to remitting bank. The condition is that the importer needs to have sufficient funds in his account in the bank.

◇ After receiving the remitter's application, the remitting bank will issue a remittance instruction or *draw a demand draft*[6] on importer's bank in the exporter's country.

◇ When the importer's bank receives the remittance instruction, it becomes the paying bank and will credit the exporter's account with the relevant amount accordingly.

◇ If it is a demand draft, the remitting bank will give the draft to the importer and the importer will provide the draft to the exporter by the importer himself. Once the exporter receives the draft, he can present it to *the nominated paying bank*[7] for the *withdrawal of payment*[8].

Types of Remittance

Depending on different form of delivering the remittance instruction from the remitting bank to the paying bank, there are three main types of remittance: mail transfer (M/T), telegraphic transfer (T/T) and demand draft (D/D).

◇ By mail transfer, after buyer hands over the payment of the goods to the remitting

149

bank, the bank will authorize its branch bank or correspondent bank (the paying bank of beneficiary) through mail to make the payment to beneficiary. This type is relatively wildly used between exporters and importers.

◇ Telegraphic transfer, different from mail transfer, means the remitting bank authorizes the paying bank through telegraphic to make the payment to beneficiary. The telegraphic could be cable, telex or *SWIFT*[9]. Comparing to mail transfer, telegraphic transfer is more expensive but it is much faster.

◇ By demand draft, the buyer will come to the local bank to buy a banker's bill and then deliver it to the seller or beneficiary by mail. After the seller or beneficiary has received it, he will come to the correspondent bank which is designated by the banker's bill to collect the money. Apart from banker's bill, promissory note or checks can also be used through this way.

Procedure and Related Parties of Collection

Collection, based on importer's commercial credit, has relatively high risk. When the banks transact collection business, they just collect the money on behalf of exporter. Therefore, checking the documents and ensuring the correct amount collected immediately are not the bank's duty. In this method, the seller is the active party but the buyer is the passive party.

In a collection transaction, there are four parties involved: principal (exporter), remitting bank (exporter's bank), collecting bank (buyer's bank) and drawee (buyer). Based on the definition of four parties, it could be clear that the procedure is different from remittance, which starts from exporter.

◇ First the exporter collects shipping documents and then draws a B/E on the importer. Then he should submit all documents with complete instructions for collection to remitting bank.

◇ After the remitting bank accepts the application, he has the duty to effect collection from the buyer. He has the duty of receiving the documents and is responsible for forwarding them to the buyer's bank along with instructions for payment.

◇ Collecting bank receives the documents from the remitting bank and presents them to the buyer for collecting cash payment or a promise to pay in the future.

◇ The last step, drawee who is the buyer owes the indicated amount. When notified by the collecting bank of the arrival of documents, the drawee has to make immediate cash payment or sign a draft according to the terms of collection order in exchange for the documents from the collecting bank.

Types of Collection

According to different shipping document attached with collection, there are three primary types of collection.

◇ Clean collection: This type is usually used when the transaction amount is small, inconvenient to provide commercial documents, such as sending samples, making up a *deficiency*[10]. Seller can conduct collection of a draft without the company of commercial documents.

◇ Documentary collection against payment (D/P): when the exporter obtains relevant commercial documents, especially the transferable transport document, it is better and securer for him to choose to effect documentary collection. Therefore, in order to get the shipping document to pick up the goods, the buyer has no choice but pay the amount immediately. When the collecting bank releases the documents to the importer only upon full and immediate cash payment, it is called documents against payment (D/P).

◇ Document collection against acceptance (D/A): D/A is only *applicable to*[11] time draft. The buyer can get the shipping documents from the collecting bank after he has accepted the draft. It is greatly convenient for the buyer, but much more risky for the seller because seller has delivered the shipping documents first, and then receive the money after a period of time. The seller might have lost this title over the goods without receiving the money yet.

Notes

1. Payment methods, that are different from paying instruments which are financial documents, are a series of activities or operations facilitating the movement of funds from one party to the other: 付款方式和付款工具不同,不是金融单据,而是一系列的把资金从一方付给另一方的操作过程
2. remittance: 汇付
3. collection: 托收
4. letter of credit: 信用证
5. favorable exchange: 顺汇。顺汇是指资金从付款一方转移到收款一方,由付款方主动汇付的方式,是国际间通过银行进行资金转移的一种方式。付款方将资金交付给当地银行,由当地银行通过与其具有业务关系的国际银行将资金付给收款方。大多是银行的汇款业务。

6. draw a demand draft：开即期汇票
7. the nominated paying bank：被指派的付款银行
8. withdrawal of payment：收款；提取付款
9. SWIFT：环球同业银行金融电讯协会。是国际银行同业间的国际合作组织，成立于1973年，是目前全球大多数国家大多数银行已使用SWIFT系统。SWIFT的使用，为银行的结算提供了安全、可靠、快捷、标准化、自动化的通讯业务，从而大大提高了银行的结算速度。
10. deficiency：不足；缺点
11. applicable to：适用于；能应用于

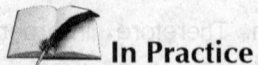

In Practice

Questions Based on the Text

I. Decide whether the following statements are true or false according to the text.

1. Payment methods that are same as paying instruments are financial documents. (   )
2. There are three main types of method: remittance, collection and letter of credit. (   )
3. Remittance is a kind of favorable exchange. (   )
4. The remitter is usually the bank. (   )
5. The remitting bank can issue a remittance before receiving the remitter's application. (   )
6. When the exporter withdraws the payment, it means he fails to collect money. (   )
7. Collection has lower risk than remittance. (   )
8. Clean collection is used when the transaction amount is small. (   )

II. Answer these questions according to the text.

1. What are the differences between payment methods and paying instruments?
2. What are the three main types of payment method?
3. What are the three parties involved in remittance?
4. What are the differences among M/T, T/T and D/D?
5. How many primary types of collection? What are they?

Chapter 7
International Payment

> **Business Vocabulary and Useful Expressions**

III. Translate the following terms.

1. favorable exchange _____
2. a demand draft _____
3. remitter _____
4. beneficiary _____
5. the nominated paying bank _____
6. mail transfer _____
7. 汇付 _____
8. 托收 _____
9. 电汇 _____
10. 商业信用 _____
11. 托收行 _____
12. 缺陷 _____

IV. Fill in the blanks with words or phrases given below. Change the form where necessary.

<u>deficiency   sufficient   favorable   nominate   withdraw</u>

1. Things will go much better if people of the same trade make up the other's _____ from their own surplus.
2. I'd like to _____ some money from my account.
3. I _____ Bill for the club president.
4. We must work hard, but equally we must get _____ rest.
5. He made several _____ comments about their candidate.

<u>a series of   telegraphic   correspondent   principal   forward</u>

6. The result was _____ with my wishes.
7. The student always asks his teacher _____ questions.
8. Please _____ my mail to my new address.
9. We commented adversely upon the imbecility of that message of _____ style.
10. The agent spoke on behalf of his _____.

> **Workshop**

V. Look at the chart below, and write down the definitions.

1. Clean collection _____

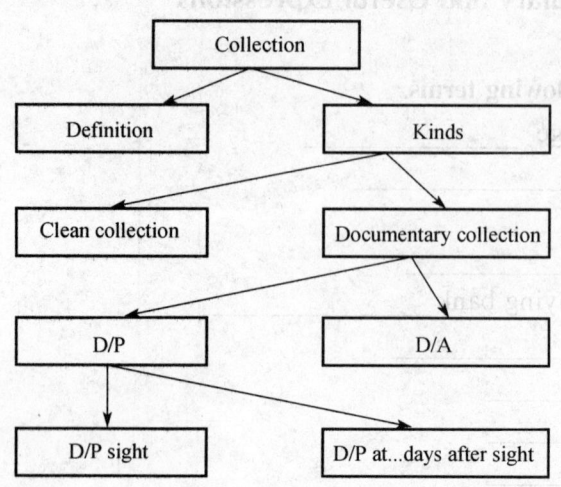

2. Documentary collection _____
3. D/P _____
4. D/A _____
5. D/P sight _____
6. D/P at ... days after sight _____

➤ Case Study

The container of goods was stolen in transit from one port to the opener's required port. If negotiating bank negotiated the documents accepted by the issuing bank to be paid on the bill's maturity as per the L/C terms and conditions.

It is unwise to get a court order barring the issuing bank from paying the negotiating bank on the maturity. Why?

3. Payment Methods of Letter of Credit

Among all the payment methods, remittance and collection are convenient but less secure to the exporter part. Therefore, they are commonly used under the circumstance of when there has already been a long-term cooperation relationship between the two parties and the both parties have a high degree of *creditability*[1]. However, before the establishment of trusting relationship, exports will worry about their successful collection of payment if they ship the goods before receiving the money. On the other hand, importers are also reluctant to pay in advance for fear of shipping delays or other problems, such as *off quality products*[2], *shortage of quantity*[3], etc. Therefore, when the exporter meets a new customer or the both parties want to have high security of transaction, it is better to choose letter of credit (L/C) as the payment method.

What Makes Letter of Credit Secure

L/C is a written commitment to pay, by a buyer's or importer's bank to the seller's or exporter's bank. A letter of credit guarantees payment of a specified sum in a specified currency, provided the seller meets *precisely-defined conditions*[4] and submits the prescribed documents within a fixed *timeframe*[5]. It means that once the seller delivers the products correctly and properly and meets all the conditions in the contract, buyer's bank has the duty to pay the exact amount to the seller after the bank receives the documents required by the credit. The buyer has no chance to delay payment.

Therefore, the most important difference of letter of credit from the other two approaches is that the security of business deal is based on bank credit rather than commercial credit. The bank, instead of buyer, takes up the payment *liability*[6] directly. Such way provides a high level protection and security to both buyers and sellers *engaged in*[7] the trade.

Related Parties of Letter of Credit

The buyer is the applicant and the seller is the beneficiary. Then, the bank that issues the L/C is referred to as the issuing bank that is also the buyer's bank. The bank that advises the L/C to the seller is called the *advising bank*[8] or *confirming bank*[9].

Procedure a Letter of Credit

◇ The contents of L/C

The credit is a completely separate document from the sales contract. The contractual relationship between the exporter and the importer does not impact on the credit operation. Therefore, the exporter should pay special attention to examining the content of the L/C document in order to avoid any conflicting items. Typically a letter of credit contains the following contents (See 7-3-1):
- Name & address of the opening bank
- Date of issuance of L/C

THE ROYAL BANK OF CANADA

BRITISH COLUMBIA INTERNATIONAL CENTRE
1055 WEST GEORGIA STREET, VANCOUVER,B.C. V6E 3P3
CANADA

CONFIRMATION OF TELEX/CABLE PRE-ADVISED　　　　　　　　　　DATE: APR 8, 1998
TELEX NO. 4720688 CA　　　　　　　　　　　　　　　　　　　　　PLACE: VANCOUVER

IRREVOCABLE DOVUMENTARY CREDIT	CREDIT NUMBER:98/0501-FTC	ADVISING BANK'S REF. NO.
ADVISING BANK: SHANGHAI A J FINACE CORPORATION 59 HANGKONG ROAD SHANGHAI 200002,CHINA	**APPLICAN:** JAMES BROWN & SONS #304-310 JALAN STREET, TORONTO, CANADA	
BENEFICIARY: HUAXIN TRADING CO., LTD. 14TH FLOOR KINGSTAR MANSION, 676 JINLIN RD., SHANGHAI CHINA	**AMOUNT:** USD46,980.00 (US DOLLARS FORTY SIX THOUSAND NINE HUNDRED AND EIGHTEEN ONLY)	
EXPIRY DATE: MAY 15, 1998　　　FOR NEGOTIATION IN APPLICANTS COUNTRY		
GENTLEMEN: WE HEREBY OPEN OUR IRREVOCABLE LETTER OF CREDIT IN YOUR FAVOR WHICH IS AVAILABLE BY YOUR DRAFTS AT SIGHT FOR FULL INVOICE VALUE ON US ACCOMPANIED BY THE FOLLOWING DOCUMENTS: +　SIGNED COMMERCIAL INVOICE AND 3 COPIES +　PACKING LIST AND 3 COPIES, SHOWING THE INDIVIDUAL WEIGHT AND MEASUREMENT OF EACH ITEM. +　ORIGINAL CERTIFICATE OF ORIGIN AND 3 COPIES ISSUED BY THE CHAMBER OF COMMERCE. +　FULL SET CLEAN ON BOARD OCEAN BILLS OF LADIG SHOWING FREIGHT PREPAID CONSIGNED TO RODER OF THE ROYAL BANK OF CANADA INDICATING THE ACTUAL DATE OF THE GOODS ON BOARD AND NOTIFY THE APPLICANT WITH FULL ADDRESS AND PHONE NO. 77009910 +　INSURANCE POLICY OR CERTIFICATE FOR 130 PERCENT OF INVOICE VALUE COVERING: INSTITUTE CARGO CLAUSES (A) AS PER I.C.C. DATED 1/1/1982. +　BENEFICIARY'S CERTIFICATE CERTIFYING THAT EACH COPY OF SHIPPING DOCUMENTS HAS BEEN FAXED TO THE APPLICANT WITHEIN 48 HOURS AFTER SHIPMENT. COVERING SHIPMENT ; 4ITEMS TEMS OF CHINESE CERAMIC DINNERWARE INCLUDING: HX1115 544SETS, HA2012 800SETS, HX4405 443SETS AND HX4510 245SETS DETAILS IN ACCORDANCE WITH SALES CONFIRMATION SHHX98027 DATED APR.3,1998. 【 】 FOB/　【 】 CFR/　【X】 CIF/　【 】 FAS TORONTO CANADA		

SHIPMENT FROM SHANGHAI	TO VANCOUVER	LATEST APRIL 30, 1998	PARTIAL SHIPMENTS PROHIBITED	TRANSSHIPMENT PROHIBITED

DRAFTS TO BE PRESENTED FOR NEGOTIATION WITHIN 15 DAYS AFTER SHIPMETN, BUT WITHIN THE VALIDITY OF CREDIT.
ALL DOCUMENTS TO BE FORWARDED IN ONE COVER, BY AIRMAIL, UNLESS OTHERWISE STATED UNDER SPECIAL INSTRUCTIONS.

SPECIAL INSTRUCTIONS: ALL BANKING CHARGES OUTSIDE CANADA ARE FOR ACCOUNT OF BENEFICIARY
+ ALL GOODS MUST BE SHIPPED IN ONE 20' CY TO CY CONTAINER AND B/L SHOWING THE SAME
+ THE VALUE OF FREIGHT PREP AID HAS TO BE SHOWN ON BILLS OF LADIG
+ DOCUMENTS WHICH FAIL TO COMPLY WITH THE TERMS AND CONDITIONS IN THE LETTER OF CREDIT SUBJECT TO A SPECIAL DISCREPANCYHANDLING FEE OF USD35.00 TO BE DEDUCTED FROM ANY PROCEEDS.

DRAFT MUST BE MARKED AS BEING DRAWN UNDER THIS CREDIT AND BEAR ITS NUMBER; THE AMOUNTS ARE TO BE ENDORSED ON THE REVERSE HEREOF BY NEG. BANK. WE HEREBY AGREE WITH THE DRAWERS, ENDORSERS AND BONA FIDE HOLDER THAT ALL DRAFTS DRAWN UNDER AND IN COMPLIANCE WITH THE TERMS OF THIS CREDIT SHALL BE DULY HONORED UPON PRESENTATION.
THIS CREDIT IS SUBJECT TO THE UNIFORM CUSTOMS AND PRACTICE FOR DOCUMENTARY CREDITS(1993 REVISION) BY THE INTERNATIONAL CHAMBER OF COMMERCE PRBLICATION NO. 500.

　　　　　DAVID JONE　　　　　　　　　　　　　　　YOURS VERY TRULY,
　　　　　　　　　　　　　　　　　　　　　　　　　　　JOANNE SUSAN
　　　AUTHORIZED SIGNATURE　　　　　　　　　　AUTHORIZED SIGNATURE

- Number of L/C
- Credit amount
- Description of goods
- Type of L/C
- Full name & address of the parties concerned
- Documents that shall be provided
- Details of shipment
- Validity period for L/C
- Settlement instructions
- Fee clauses
- Special clause, if any

◇ *Issuance*[10], amendment and *utilization*[11] of Letter of Credit

Normally, there are three procedures: issuance, amendment and utilization.

Issuance: In this performance, seller and buyer negotiate the details of L/C.

(1) Both two parties, the buyer and the seller have agreed on the terms of sale: specifying a documentary credit as the means of payment; choosing an advising bank (usually it is the seller's bank); listing required documents.

(2) The buyer applies to issuing bank and opens a documentary credit which names the seller the beneficiary based on specific terms and conditions that are listed in the credit.

(3) The issuing bank sends the documentary credit to the advising bank named in the credit.

(4) The advising bank informs the seller of the documentary credit.

Amendment: Some times, after an L/C is issued, seller might have other needs to revise the document. Then he has to apply for the amendment.

(1) The seller requests that the buyer make an amendment to the credit through a telephone call, a fax letter, or by face-to-face negotiation.

(2) If the buyer agrees, the buyer orders the issuing bank to issue the amendment.

(3) The issuing bank amends the credit and notifies the advising bank of the proposed amendment.

(4) The advising bank notifies seller of the amendment.

Utilization: Once there is no *dissidence*[12] of the document credit, exporter ships the products, and based on the bank's credit, buyer collects the amount.

（1）The beneficiary ships the goods to the buyer and obtains a negotiable transport document, such as bill of lading, from the shipping agent.

（2）The seller collects and presents a document package to the advising bank, including the negotiable transport document and other documents (e.g. commercial invoice, insurance document, certificate of origin, inspection certificate) as required by the buyer in the documentary credit.

（3）After the whole set of documents is presented to the exporter's bank, the bank will perform some document checking to ensure their compliance with the terms of the documentary credit. Once the documents are fine, the advising bank pays the seller based upon the terms of the credit.

（4）The advising bank sends the documentation package by mail or by express to the issuing bank.

（5）The issuing bank reviews the document package. After the bank is sure about the documents are in conformity with the terms of the credit, the amount is paid to the advising bank based upon the terms of the credit. Then the issuing bank advises the buyer that the documents have arrived.

（6）The buyer reviews the document package and pays the sum to issuing bank through cash payment, sight draft or collection, etc.

（7）The issuing bank sends the document package by mail or express to the buyer who is the processor of the shipment.

Notes

1. creditability：信用度
2. off quality products：劣质产品
3. shortage of quantity：数量短缺
4. precisely-defined conditions：明确的条款
5. timeframe：时间范围
6. liability：责任；债务人
7. engaged in：陷入于……；从事于……
8. advising bank：通知行
9. confirming bank：确认行
10. issuance：发行
11. utilization：应用；利用
12. dissidence：异议

Chapter 7
International Payment

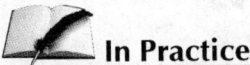
In Practice

> ### Questions Based on the Text

I. Decide whether the following statements are true or false according to the text.
1. Buyers are reluctant to pay in advance for fear of shipping delays or other problems, such as off quality products, shortage of quantity.　　(　)
2. L/C is a commitment to pay, written by a buyer or importer.　　(　)
3. If the seller delivers the products correctly and properly and meets all the conditions in the contract, buyer still could cancel the payment.　　(　)
4. Once the issuing bank opens a documentary credit, L/C is non-modifiable.　(　)
5. Usually, the beneficiary is the buyer.　　(　)
6. After the goods are shipped, seller has the duty to present the shipping documents to the advising bank.　　(　)
7. The party who sends the documentation package to the issuing bank is buyer.　　(　)
8. Usually, buyer has to pay the sum to issuing bank after he reviews the document package.　　(　)

II. Answer these questions according to the text.
1. What's the advantage of L/C? Why both of two parties, buyer and seller, can obtain benefits from it?
2. How many types of bank are related in one L/C case?
3. What are the main contents of L/C?
4. What is the procedure of issuance?
5. What is the procedure of utilization?

> ### Business Vocabulary and Useful Expressions

III. Translate the following terms.
1. creditability ＿＿＿＿＿＿＿＿＿
2. trusting relationship ＿＿＿＿＿＿＿＿＿
3. high security of transaction ＿＿＿＿＿＿＿＿＿
4. precisely-defined conditions ＿＿＿＿＿＿＿＿＿

159

5. issuing bank _____
6. utilization _____
7. 数量短缺 _____
8. 劣质产品 _____
9. 时间范围 _____
10. 达到合同中的要求 _____
11. 申请人 _____
12. 通知行 _____

IV. Fill in the blanks with words or phrases given below. Change the form where necessary.

creditability shortage precisely liability engaged in

1. Power _____ browned out the city that winter.
2. The judge exempted them from all _____ in these matters.
3. The professor is _____ advanced studies.
4. That answers _____ to our need.
5. Such fundamentals having wide acceptance give reliability and _____ to the financial statements prepared by the accountants.

confirm conflict issuance amendment dissidence

6. Both sides suffered heavy casualties in the border armed _____.
7. This certificate expires 180 days after _____.
8. The treaty was _____ by the president.
9. The interested party may apply for _____ registration, in case the holder recorded in the realty register does not agree to the alteration.
10. The _____ is an appendage of that contract.

➤ Workshop

V. Read the text again, and write down each bank's duty.
   A. opens a documentary credit
   B. sends the documentary credit to another bank
   C. informs the seller of the documentary credit
   D. amends the credit and notifies another bank
   E. notifies seller of the amendment
   F. perform some document checking to ensure their compliance with the terms of the documentary credit

G. pays the seller based upon the terms of the credit
H. sends the documentation package by mail or by express to another bank
1. Advising bank _____.
2. Issuing bank _____.

> **Case Study**

FF Company signed a contract to export goods to AA company in Africa. In September, FF was notified of the L/C, but the money of account was different from that required by the sales contract. Besides, the goods were not ready for shipment. In November, AA urged FF to deliver the goods. FF requested an L/C amendment and an extension of the shipment date. The next day, AA cabled back, "L/C amended." FF shipped the goods. However, the amended L/C never arrived, and the opening bank refused to pay against the shipping documents. The goods were stored in the warehouse at the port of destination. FF had to pay much rent and insurance. At this time, AA requested D/A.

Should FF accept it? Is there any lesson to be learnt from this case?

Chapter 8

Inspection, Claim, Force Majeure and Arbitration

In international trade practice, some necessary clauses such as *commodity inspection clause*[1], matters of claim, force majeure and arbitration are usually stipulated in the contract to avoid any dispute and trouble between the exporter and the importer.

1. Commodity Inspection

Inspection is considered to be *an indispensable step*[2] in the process of commodity transportation. It is not difficult at all to understand why both an importer and an exporter want to inspect the goods.

For the importer, *he wants to make certain that the delivered goods he is purchasing are exactly the ones described by the contract he has signed with the seller*[3]. For the exporter, he wants to control the quality of the goods so that his reputation will not be damaged and get the payment smoothly. And what's more, he can *expand the market*[4] due to the excellent quality of the delivered goods.

Commodity inspection, therefore, is considered to be absolutely necessary in the process of commodity transportation to protect the interests of both the importer and the exporter.

Time and Place for Inspection

The time and place in which the inspection is to be made differ from country to country. Generally speaking, the time and place *are closely related to*[5] the trade terms and the nature of commodity of a contract, the industry *customs and practice*[6] and the state's statue etc. The manner in which inspection is to be made can be outlined as the following.

◇ Inspection at the factory

The inspection is to be made, because of the dispatch of the goods at the factory, by an authorized party, as required by the contract, or by both the inspector of the factory and the inspector of the buyer. It is also called *shipping quality and weight*[7]. *Risks in transit in respect of the quality and the quantity of the goods shall be borne by the buyer*[8]. This one is more favorable to the seller.

◇ Inspection at *the port of destination*[9]

It is also referred to as *landed quality and weight*[10]. The weight certificate and the quality certificate issued by the *inspection authority*[11] at the port of destination shall be used as the final evidence for the weight and the quality of the contracted goods. Obviously, this method is favorable to the buyer. This kind of approach is widely accepted by the traders who are dealing with *bulk commodities*[12].

◇ Inspection at *the port of shipment*[13] and re-inspection at the port of destination

Certificate issued by the inspection authority at the port of shipment shall be one of the documents to be presented by the seller to the bank for negotiation, but shall not be the final proof for the quality and weight of the goods. On the other hand, re-inspection shall be made at the agreed time by the agreed inspection authority at the port of destination.

In case the quality or weight of the goods is found to *be inconsistent with*[14] the contract, and such an inconsistency is caused by the seller, then the re-inspection certificate can be used as final evidence by the buyer for the *recovering damages from*[15] the seller. Since this kind of method *benefits for*[16] both parties *to a certain degree*[17], it is widely used in international trade.

Inspection Authority

There are mainly two types of inspection body: governmental and non-governmental. The governmental inspection bodies are owned or supervised by governments, such as *the General Administration of Quality Supervision, Inspection and Quarantine of the People's Republic of China (GAQSIQ) in our country, the Food and Drug Administration (FDA) in the USA specialize in inspection of particular merchandise*[18] (grain, drug, etc.).

The international inspection of commodity is mainly run by individuals or trade associations upon application by the seller or the buyer, such as *the Society General De Surveillance S.A. (SGS) in Geneva, Swiss, Underwriter Laboratory (UL) in the USA*[19], etc. The surveyors execute inspection or analysis over the export or import commodities as to their quality, weight, quantity, packaging, marking, and place of origin or damage.

Inspection Standard

Inspection on import and export commodities performed by the commodity inspection authorities shall cover quality, specifications, quantity, weight, packing and *the requirements for safety and hygiene*[20]. The commodity inspection authorities shall conduct inspection according to the following standards.

◇ The *compulsory standards*[21]

If the compulsory standards or other inspection standards which must be complied with are specified by *law or administrative regulation*[22], the inspection shall be performed according to the standards as specified by laws and administrative regulation.

◇ Standards in the international trade contracts

If there are no relevant compulsory standards or other inspection standards which must be complied with as specified by law or administrative regulations, the inspection shall be performed according to the standards agreed upon in the international trade contracts. If the trade is conducted against the sample, the inspection shall be performed simultaneously according to the sample provided. In the process of inspection, the higher standard should be conducted. And if there is not any inspection standard for the goods, the standards of the manufacturing country shall be conducted.

Inspection Certificate

After the inspection of the goods, the inspection authority will issue inspection certificates, which are written documents to *bear witness to*[23] the results of inspection. It is used to verify whether the goods are in conformity with the terms of contract. If the verification is positive, the certificates are the documents for payment while if not, they are the documents for refusal of the goods and *claim for compensation*[24].

Most frequently used certificates are:
- Inspection Certificate of Quality
- Inspection Certificate of Weight
- Inspection Certificate of Quantity
- Inspection Certificate of Value
- Inspection Certificate of Origin

- Sanitary Inspection Certificate
- Veterinary Inspection Certificate
- Disinfection Inspection Certificate
- *Inspection Certificate on Damaged Cargo*[25]

Inspection Clause

In order to clarify the inspection or reinspection time, place, authority, the inspection items and the inspection certificates required, it is necessary to set down the inspection clause in the contract.

The following is a sample of inspection clause for the cargo in an import contract:

"Before making delivery, the manufacturers shall make an inspection of the goods. After arrival of the goods at the port/place of destination, the buyer shall have the right to reinspect the quality and weight of the cargo."

Notes

1. commodity inspection clause：商品检验条款
2. an indispensable step：一个不可缺少的步骤
3. He wants to make certain that the delivered goods he is purchasing are exactly the ones described by the contract he has signed with the seller：他想确定要发送的货物，也就是自己购买的货物是否同卖家签订合同时描述的产品是完全一致的
4. expand the market：扩大市场，拓销
5. are closely related to：与……有密切关系
6. customs and practice：惯例和习惯做法
7. shipping quality and weight：离岸品质和离岸重量
8. Risks in transit in respect of the quality and the quantity of the goods shall be borne by the buyer：关于货物质量和数量在运输途中的风险由买家承担
9. the port of destination：目的港
10. landed quality and weight：到岸质量和到岸重量
11. inspection authority：检验机构
12. bulk commodities：大宗商品；散装货
13. the port of shipment：运输港
14. be inconsistent with：与……不一致
15. recovering damages from：挽回损失

16. benefits for：对……有利
17. to a certain degree：在一定程度上
18. The General Administration of Quality Supervision, Inspection and Quarantine of the People's Republic of China（GAQSIQ）in our country, the Food and Drug Administration （FDA） in the USA specialize in inspection of particular merchandise：在我国的中国质量监督检验和检疫管理局，专门检验特殊商品的美国食品药物管理局
19. the Society General De Surveillance S. A.（SGS）in Geneva, Swiss, Underwriter Laboratory（UL）in the USA：瑞士日内瓦通用鉴定公司和美国保险人实验室
20. the requirements for safety and hygiene：对安全卫生的要求
21. compulsory standards：强制性标准
22. law or administrative regulation：法律或行政法规
23. bear witness to：作证
24. claim for compensation：索赔
25. Sanitary Inspection Certificate, Veterinary Inspection Certificate, Disinfection Inspection Certificate, Inspection Certificate on Damaged Cargo：卫生检验证书、兽医检验证书、消毒检验证书、残缺货物检验证书

In Practice

➢ Questions Based on the Text

I. Decide whether the following statements are true or false according to the text.

1. In international trade, inspection of commodity and the issuance of certificate of inspection are necessary steps in the transfer of the goods.　　　　　　（　）
2. Under the mode of shipping quality and weight, both parties agree that the commodities are inspected before shipping, and the resulting inspection certificate serve as final proof of the quality and weight of the commodities.　　　　（　）
3. Inspection at the port of destination is undoubtedly beneficial to the seller and is disadvantageous to the buyer.　　　　　　　　　　　　　　　　　　（　）
4. The Society General De Surveillance S. A.（SGS）in Geneva, Swiss is governmental inspection authority.　　　　　　　　　　　　　　　　　　　　　　（　）
5. Because of a variety of areas that may be covered under inspection, commodity inspection certificates are of many corresponding types.　　　　　　　　（　）
6. In the absence of the compulsory standards or other inspection standards, the

inspection shall be conducted according to the sample. ( )
7. Inspection certificate can be used to prove whether the quality, weight or packing etc. of the goods delivered by the seller is in accordance with the contract. ( )
8. To clarify the responsibilities between the seller and the buyer, inspection clauses are usually stipulated in the contract. ( )

II. Answer these questions according to the text.
1. Does the seller want to inspect the goods? Why?
2. What are the ways to stipulate the place and time of inspection?
3. How many types of inspection body are there? Give an example for each one.
4. How many kinds of inspection certificates do you know?
5. Why should the inspection clause be stipulated in the contract?

> **Business Vocabulary and Useful Expressions**

III. Translate the following terms.
1. expand the market _____
2. customs and practice _____
3. the port of destination _____
4. make certain _____
5. shipping quality _____
6. 检验机构 _____
7. 对……有利 _____
8. 商品检验条款 _____
9. 到岸重量 _____
10. 大宗商品 _____
11. 强制性标准 _____
12. 作证 _____

IV. Fill in the blanks with words or phrases given below. Change the form where necessary.

| indispensable outline dispatch negotiation inconsistency |

1. Taking care of my parents is my _____ duty.
2. They closed the deal in sugar after a week of _____.
3. They _____ their projects for rebuilding their hometown after the flooding.
4. Please advise us of the _____ of the goods when the goods are prepared.

5. _____ between the selling price and the amount of received gold has been fixed.

> supervise   execute   hygiene   compulsory   administrative

6. Some subjects, such as mathematice, physics and English, are _____ for the students in this department.
7. Develop and manage Request for Quotation (RFQ) and _____ evaluation process.
8. People are now paying attention to cleanliness and personal _____.
9. The Special _____ Region will pass its own legislation.
10. Furthermore, the system can _____ the pollution-emission activities through insurance company.

> what's more   expand the market   be inconsistent with   recover from   specialize in

11. To _____ is one of the key links in developing the economy.
12. It took a long time for him to _____ a bad cold.
13. The results of the experiment _____ his prediction.
14. This company founded in 2002, _____ heavy trucks and related parts and components.
15. He can speak English, and _____ he speaks it very well.

➢ Workshop

V. **Match each term with the correct definition, the first one is given.**

Term	Definition
Inspection Certificates	This certifies that the quality and specifications of import and export commodities are in conformity with the contract stipulation.
Inspection Certificate of Quality	It indicates the inspection conducted by an authorized party within the time period stipulated in the sales contact at the port of destination.
Landed Quality and Weight	This certifies the degree to which the goods imported have been damaged and the causes of the damage
Inspection Certificate on Damaged Cargo	They, which are written documents in foreign trade practice, certify the result of commodity inspection issued by an inspection institution.
Inspection Clause	It contains stipulations on the inspection right, the time and place or re-inspection time, authority, the inspection items and the inspection certificates.

168

Chapter 8
Inspection, Claim, Force Majeure and Arbitration

> **Case Study**

One company in China imported a batch of pine timber from an American company. The inspection clause stipulated in the contract is shipping quality and weight. The inspection standard should be in accordance with the Western Standard of America. When the goods arrived at the port of destination, the Chinese company found that some parts of the goods were damaged in transit.

Who should be responsible for the damage, the Chinese company or the American company? Why?

2. Claim

In international trade, when one party fails to fulfill his obligations stipulated in the contract and causes the other party *financial losses*[1], the latter would demand the former to compensate him for the losses. Claim can be defined as a demand made by one party upon another for a certain amount of payment *on account of*[2] a loss sustained through its negligence.

For example, if the importer found the goods were in bad quality when they arrived, he could *make a claim against the exporter for compensation*[3].

Breach of Contract

Breach of contract[4] means the refusal or failure by a party to a contract to fulfill an obligation as stipulated in the contract. In international trade transaction, either the seller or the buyer may break the sales contract.

A seller may be considered to have breached a contract:
- The seller fails to deliver the goods on time.
- The documents relating to goods are incomplete.
- The goods do not conform to the contract.

A buyer may be considered to have breached a contract:
- The buyer fails to pay the price within the stipulated period.
- The buyer fails to take delivery of the goods.

Liabilities of Breach of Contract

The party, the seller or the buyer, may *take responsibility for*[5] breaching a contract because he may misunderstand or misinterpret the clauses of contract that are not clearly or definitely stipulated, which is likely to *give rise to disputes*[6]. Different legal systems differ in their definition of breach of contract

◇ **Fundamental breach and non-fundamental breach**[7].

According to *the United Nations Convention on Contracts for the International Sale of Goods*（*CISG*）[8], there are two types of breach of contract: fundamental breach and non-fundamental breach.

CISG Article 25 provides that "*A breach of contract committed by one of the parties is fundamental if it results in such to the other party as substantially to deprive him of what he is entitled to expect under the contract, unless the party in breach did not foresee and a reasonable person in the same circumstances would not have foreseen such a result*"[9]. The injured party may declare the contract void and claim damages.

In the case of a non-fundamental breach of contract, the party suffering the losses can only claim damages but not *declare the contract void*[10].

Whether a term in the contract is a fundamental term, going to the root of the contract, or only a non-fundamental term, entitling *an aggrieved party*[11] to damages only, depends upon the statements made by the parties concerned at the time. If it is made clear by one party that he regards a particular term as vital, it will usually be regarded as a Fundamental Breach.

◇ **Breach of condition and breach of warranty**[12]

The British law divides the breach of contract into breach of condition and breach of warranty.

Breach of condition refers to the breach of the major terms of the contract, such as quality, quantity (weight), name of goods, package manners, price amount and so on; the suffering party may declare the contract void and claim damages.

Breach of warranty means breach of the minor terms of the contract, the breach of which gives rise to a claim for damages, but not to a right to reject the goods and treat the contract as repudiated.

For example, the quality and quantity of the goods delivered by the seller don't conform to stipulation of contract, or the goods are not delivered according to the stipulated date in the contract. In these cases, the injured party is entitled to discharge the contract and raise claim against the other party. If the violated clauses are major ones, such a breach is called "breach of condition" while it is called "breach of warranty" if the terms are minor.

Claim Clause in Contract

As is known to all, the last stage in international trade procedure is *settlement of* disputes[13]. Even though it is not necessarily a step for every transaction in international trade, disputes between the seller and the buyer are very common.

In order to avoid or to properly handle future disputes, a claim clause is usually contained in the sales contract. There are normally two ways to stipulate claim clause in the contract: *discrepancy and claim clause and penalty clause*[14].

◇ Discrepancy and claim clause

This is the commonly adopted claim clause in an international sales contract to guard against that the quality or package of the goods delivered is inconsistent with the contract. It also includes, besides stipulating that if any party breaches a contract the other party is entitled to *lodge claim against the party in breach*[15], other aspects in respect of proofs presented when lodging a claim and effective period for filing a claim etc.

The evidence or proof provided should be complete and clear and the relevant certificates issued by the authority should be competent to support the claim. Otherwise, the claims can be refused by the other party. Proofs include legal proof which refers to the sales contract and the *relevant governing laws and regulations*[16] and fact proof which refers to the facts and the relevant written evidence in respect of the breach.

Here is an example:

> Any knowledge or information concerning the design, manufacture, sale or use of the items covered by this order which seller may disclose to buyer *incident to the performance, manufacture or delivery of items covered by this order*[18] shall be deemed to have been disclosed as a deliverable under the order and to be free from all restrictions as to the use or disposition thereof by buyer, and seller agrees not to *assert any claim against buyer*[19] by reason of Buyer's use or disposition thereof. Seller shall keep confidential all information, drawings, specifications, data or any other details furnished by buyer or prepared by seller specifically in connection with this order.

◇ Penalty clause

Most of the contracts contain only discrepancy and claim clause, but contracts for bulk commodities or machines and equipment will include not only discrepancy and claim clause, but also penalty clause.

Under this clause, the party who fails to deliver the goods on time or fails to make payment on time, must pay another party a fine, a certain percentage of total contract value. The *penalty ceiling*[19] should be included in the contract.

Two examples of penalty clause are as the follows:

> Any defective part received at Company A will incur a $280 USD[20] indirect cost plus any direct cost of material and labor ($75 USD per hour).

> For any delay in shipment a penalty of 2.5% of the value of shipment per week or part thereof up to maximum of 5% is to be deducted from any amount payable in respect of such shipment. Such deduction should be shown in the invoices.

Notes

1. financial losses：经济损失
2. on account of：由于；基于
3. make a claim against the exporter for compensation：向出口商提出了索赔
4. breach of contract：违反合同；违约
5. take responsibility for：为……负责任
6. give rise to dispute：引起争端
7. fundamental breach and non-fundamental breach：重大违约和轻微违约
8. the United Nations Convention on Contracts for the International Sale of Goods (CISG)：联合国国际货物销售合同公约
9. A breach of contract committed by one of the parties is fundamental if it results in such to the other party as substantially to deprive him of what he is entitled to expect under the contract, unless the party in breach did not foresee and a reasonable person in the same circumstances would not have foreseen such a result：一方当事人违反合同的结果，若使另一方当事人蒙受损失，以至于实际剥夺了他根据合同规定有权期待得到的东西，即为根本违反合同，除非违反合同一方并不预知一个同等资格、通情达理的人处于相同情况中也没有理由预知会发生这样的结果
10. declare the contract void：宣布合同作废
11. an aggrieved party：受损害的一方
12. breach of condition and breach of warranty：违反要件和违反担保
13. settlement of disputes：解决争端
14. discrepancy and claim clause and penalty clause：异议与索赔条款和罚金条款
15. lodge claim against the party in breach：对违约一方提出索赔
16. relevant governing laws and regulations：相关的政府法律法规

17. incident to the performance, manufacture or delivery of items covered by this order: 附随订单里包括的产品的性能、加工或者交货期
18. assert any claim against buyer: 向买方要求索赔
19. penalty ceiling: 赔付最高限额
20. Any defective part received at Company A will incur a ＄280 USD: 任何发到 A 公司的次品都将被要求赔款，每个 280 美金

In Practice

> ## Questions Based on the Text

I. Decide whether the following statements are true or false according to the text.
1. Breach of a contract arises where any party of a contract does not abide by the stipulations of the contract. ( )
2. Breach of contract committed by the seller may result from the delay of issuing the L/C. ( )
3. Condition terms are ones of the contract to which the parties, when making the contract, attach such importance that they can truly be described as being of the essence of the contract. ( )
4. If a breach of contract by a party is non-fundamental, then the injured part is entitled to recover damages from the party in breach and cancel the contract. ( )
5. Any party, either the seller or the buyer, who has violated the contract, shall be legally held responsible for the breach. ( )
6. If the proofs are not complete and clear, the claims could be refused by the other part. ( )
7. For transactions where goods in substantial quantity are concerned, only a penalty clause will be stipulated in the contract. ( )
8. The penalty ceiling is the maximum amount of the fine paid to the injured party. ( )

II. Answer these questions according to the text.
1. What is a claim?
2. What are the reasons that result in disputes for the sellers in international trade?
3. According to the British law, what can the breach of contract be divided?

4. How many ways to stipulate claim clause are there in the contract? What are they?
5. What kind of contract often contains penalty clause?

➤ **Business Vocabulary and Useful Expressions**

1. financial losses _____
2. breach of contract _____
3. deprive ... of _____
4. an aggrieved party _____
5. settlement of disputes _____
6. lodge claim against the party in breach _____
7. 为……负责任 _____
8. 引起争端 _____
9. 重大违约 _____
10. 宣布合同作废 _____
11. 赔付最高限额 _____
12. 异议与索赔条款 _____

IV. Fill in the blanks with words or phrases given below. Change the form where necessary.

sustain   negligence   breach   misinterpret   fundamental

1. Now the cheers and applause mingled in a single _____ roar.
2. A trivial misunderstanding caused a _____ of contract.
3. There is nothing of the kind in what they said; you always try to _____ the words of others.
4. The _____ cause of the development of a thing lies in its internal contradictoriness.
5. Many a customer has been lost through _____ of service.

foresee   void   aggrieve   warranty   incur

6. The agreement will be considered null and _____.
7. The _____ parties ought to perform their own investigation and show their evidence.
8. The purchaser of this automobile is protected by the manufacturer's _____.
9. He could never have _____ that one day his books would sell in million.
10. An enterprise has to _____ certain costs and expenses in order to stay in business.

Chapter 8
Inspection, Claim, Force Majeure and Arbitration

| financial losses | make a claim against | relate to |
| take responsibility for | be entitled to | |

11. Why can't people _____ their actions anymore?
12. The buyer had no intention to _____ the seller when the reason of delay delivery was given.
13. Now we will hear news _____ companies and stock markets.
14. Because of this failure, daily a large amount of waste, resulting in considerable _____.
15. If one side fails to honor the contract, the other side _____ cancel it.

➢ Workshop

Please translate all the clauses into Chinese and discuss with your partner and see what items the clauses are about.

> Any claim by the buyers on the goods shipped shall be filed within 30 days after the arrival of the goods at the port of destination and supported by a survey report issued by a surveyor approved by the sellers. Claims in respect of matters within responsibility of the insurance company and/or shipping company will not be considered or entertained by the sellers.

> In case of delayed delivery, the sellers shall pay to the buyers for every week of delay a penalty that amounts to 0.5% of the total value of the goods whose delivery has been delayed. Any fractional part of a week is to be considered a full week. The total amount of penalty shall not, however, exceed 5% of the total value of the goods involved in late delivery and be to be deducted from the price amount by the bank at the time of negotiation, or by the buyers directly at the time of payment.

175

Any discrepancy about quality should be presented within 30 days after the arrival of the goods at the port of destination; any discrepancy about quantity should be presented within 15 days after the arrival of the goods at the port of destination, both of which cases should be on the strength of the certificates issued by the related surveyor. If the seller is liable, he should send the reply together with the proposal for settlement within 20 days after receiving the said discrepancy.

➢ Case Study

Read the following letter of claim carefully and find out:

1. Why did the buyer make a claim?
2. How much should the seller pay according to the letter?

> Dear Sirs
> The captioned goods you shipped per S.S. "Yellow River" on May 14 arrived here yesterday.
> On examination, we have found that many of the sewing machines are severely damaged, though the cases themselves show no trace of damage.
> An investigation made by the surveyor has revealed the fact that the damage is attributable to improper packing. For further particulars, we refer you to the surveyor's report enclosed.
> We are therefore, compelled to claim on you to compensate us for the loss, $27,500, which we have sustained by the damage to the goods.
> We trust that you will be kind enough to accept this claim and deduct the sum claimed from the amount of your next invoice to us.
> Sincerely,
> Grace

3. Force Majeure

Definition of Force Majeure

Force majeure, also called Art of God, is an event which can generally be neither *anticipated nor brought under control*[1], as a result of which the party is unable to perform its obligations under this contract, such as an earthquake, an industrial strike, and a war etc.

When these events take place, it may be impossible for the parties involved to fulfill the contract. A party *is not liable for any loss or damage*[2] resulting from his failure to perform the contract caused by force majeure.

However, at first, he must prove that the failure was *due to an impediment beyond his control*[3] and that he could not reasonably be expected to have *taken the impediment into account*[4] at the time of the conclusion of the contract or to have avoided or overcome it or its consequences.

A force majeure event should have the following features.
- It happens after the contract is signed.
- It is not due to negligence of the buyer or the seller.
- Neither the buyer nor the seller can control the situation.

The stipulation of force majeure in the sales contract enables a seller to avoid his contractual obligations without paying a compensation or penalty. Of course, *the party claiming force majeure has the burden to prove the direct relationship between the force majeure and the non-performance of its obligations under this contract*[5].

The party claiming inability to perform its obligations due to an event of force majeure shall *take appropriate measures to minimize or remove the effects*[6] of the event of force majeure and within the shortest possible time, do its best to *resume performance of the obligation*[7] affected by the event force majeure.

Consequences of Force Majeure

Generally speaking, there are two consequences of force majeure: *termination of the contract and postponement of the contract*[8]. Whether terminating the contract or postponing the performance of the contract *depends on*[9] what degree the force majeure event has affected the performance of the contract, or on the detailed stipulations in the contract.

◇ Termination of the contract

In the cases of natural disasters or other events that have made it impossible to fulfill the contract, one of the parties who suffers the force majeure event may ask for the termination of the contract.

For example, an earthquake has destroyed the goods that is being shipped or destroyed the manufacturing factory, and then the contract can be terminated.

◇ Postponement of the contract

When the performance of the contract is *delayed temporarily*[10], the contract can be postponed but not terminated since it is still possible for the seller to carry out his contractual obligations.

For example, if the transportation is delayed by a hurricane temporarily, the contract has to suspend. But when the hurricane is over, the goods should be shipped *without any delay*[11].

In a word, the contract can be avoided only if the occurrence of the force majeure event makes it impossible to perform the contract, such as the loss of or damage to specifically *designated goods*[12], or the event is so serious that it is impossible to recover within a short period of time. Otherwise, the suffering party can only postpone the performance of the contract to *reduce the possible losses*[13] to the other party.

Force Majeure Clause in the Contract

A force majeure clause usually contains *the scope of force majeure, time limit of notifying the other party and the issuer of the certificates*[14].

◇ The scope of force majeure event

Since there is no definite explanation as to which events should be regarded as force majeure, the kinds of events should *be specified as clearly as possible*[15] by both the seller and the buyer.

For instance, some people include *social disturbances or strikes*[16] as force majeure events, but some other people disagree. If the scope of the events is not clearly defined, there might be difficulties in using the clause.

Generally, there are basically three ways to set the scope the natural disasters:
- General stipulation: "generally recognized force majeure causes".
- Specific listing: "war, flood, storm, heavy snow".
- Specific listing plus general stipulation: "war, flood, storm, heavy snow or any other causes beyond their control and other generally recognized force majeure causes".

◇ Time limit of notifying the other party

In case of a force majeure event, the suffering party who fails to perform the contact

Chapter 8
Inspection, Claim, Force Majeure and Arbitration

must give notice to the other party of the impediment and its effect on his ability to perform. If the notice is not received by the other party *within a reasonable time*[17], the suffering party will still be liable for the loss or *extended loss caused*[18].

◇ **The issuer of the certificate**

A force majeure should be verified by government authorities or a *chamber of commerce*[19] at the location where the event takes place. The issuer of the certificate or report may be specified in the clause.

Here is an example of a force majeure clause in the international sales contract:

Force Majeure.

Neither party is liable for failure to perform, except *with respect to*[20] payment obligations, solely caused by:
- unavoidable casualty
- *embargoes*[21]
- government orders
- acts of civil or military authorities
- acts by common carriers, emergency conditions (including weather conditions) *incompatible with*[22] safety or good quality workmanship, or any similar unforeseen event that renders performance commercially *implausible*[23].

If an event of force majeure occurs, the party experiencing the force majeure circumstances shall inform the injured party by cable or telex and furnish the latter within 15 days by registered airmail with a certificate issued by the competent government authorities. The party experiencing the force majeure circumstances shall cooperate with and assist the injured party *in all reasonable ways*[24] to minimize the impact of force majeure on the injured party, which may include locating and arranging substitute services if necessary.

Notes

1. Force majeure, also called Art of God, is an event can generally be neither anticipated nor brought under control: 不可抗力,又称上帝之为,是一种无法预见也无法控制的事故

2. is not liable for any loss or damage: 对一切损失或者损坏不承担责任

3. due to an impediment beyond his control：源于无法控制的事故障碍
4. taken the impediment into account：把该事故障碍考虑进去
5. the party claiming force majeure has the burden to prove the direct relationship between the force majeure and the non-performance of its obligations under this contract：面临不可抗力的一方有责任证明不可抗力和无法履行合同义务之间有着直接的关系
6. take appropriate measures to minimize or remove the effects：采取恰当的措施把影响降到最低或者消除影响
7. resume performance of the obligation：重新履行义务
8. termination of the contract and postponement of the contract：终止合同的和延期合同
9. depends on：由……决定；取决于……
10. delayed temporarily：暂时延误
11. without any delay：立即，马上
12. designated goods：指定的货物
13. reduce the possible losses：减低所有可能的损失
14. the scope of force majeure, time limit of notifying the other party and the issuer of the certificates：不可抗力的范围，通知另一方的时间限制和证明开具方
15. be specified as clearly as possible：尽可能清楚地描述
16. social disturbances or strikes：社会动乱或罢工
17. within a reasonable time：在合理的时间内
18. extended loss caused：引起的更多的损失
19. chamber of commerce：商会
20. with respect to：关于
21. embargoes：禁运
22. incompatible with：与……冲突，不符
23. implausible：难以置信的，不可能的
24. in all reasonable ways：以所有合理的方式

# In Practice

➢ Questions Based on the Text

I. Decide whether the following statements are true or false according to the text.

1. Force majeure means an event beyond the control of a party, as a result of which the

party is unable to perform its obligations under this contract.   (   )
2. Certain natural disasters and social disturbances are considered force majeure.   (   )
3. Whether a specific event is considered force majeure or not depends on the injured party.   (   )
4. A force majeure clause could be signed after the specific event happened.   (   )
5. Due to the force majeure can not be controlled by both parties, even if the party experiencing the force majeure could not inform the other party, he is not liable for any loss or damage resulting from his failure to perform the contract.   (   )
6. A force majeure event should be verified by a certificate or survey report that attests such an event.   (   )
7. If the occurrence of force majeure event has damaged or destroyed the basic of the contract and makes it impossible to perform the contract, then the contract can only be terminated.   (   )
8. It is a protection clause for the seller to enable him to avoid obligations without paying compensation.   (   )

II. Answer these questions according to the text.
1. What is force majeure?
2. What are some of the major features of a force majeure event?
3. Who will decide the scope of force majeure events?
4. On what situation will the contract be terminated?
5. What factors need to be considered when drafting the force majeure clause?

> Business Vocabulary and Useful Expressions

III. Translate the following terms.
1. force majeure _____
2. beyond his control _____
3. take appropriate measures _____
4. resume performance of the obligation _____
5. without any delay _____
6. take ... into account _____
7. 延期合同 _____
8. 指定的货物 _____
9. 社会动乱 _____

10. 与……冲突，不符 _____
11. 不可抗力的范围 _____
12. 商会 _____

IV. **Fill in the blanks with words or phrases given below. Change the form where necessary.**

anticipate   impediment   feature   minimize   termination

1. Funding gaps for smaller firms are a major _____ to growth.
2. The most striking _____ of this graph is the lack of agreement.
3. Failure to comply with these conditions will result in _____ of the contract.
4. You can _____ the dangers of driving by taking care to obey the rules of the road.
5. Do you often try to _____ what your child will do and forestall problems?

temporarily   occurrence   notify   disturbance   implausible

6. Soldiers had _____ closed the border between the two countries.
7. We'll _____ the time of the meeting on the bulletin board.
8. During the _____ which followed, three Englishmen were hurt.
9. Predictions that Japan would overtake the America, popular in the late 1980s, were always _____.
10. The _____ of storms delayed our trip.

take ... into account   contractual obligation   without any delay
depend on   incompatible with

11. Problems, if any, should be solved _____.
12. Every _____ in a contract gives rise to a corresponding contractual right.
13. Needy and handicapped people _____ government relief for their support.
14. When we are speaking of power, time is _____.
15. Excessive drinking is _____ good health.

> **Workshop**

When negotiating force majeure clauses, make sure the clause applies equally to all parties. Be sure to include specific examples of events that will excuse performance under the clause. Please find out the events which are the force majeure from the following events.

A

A. earthquakes
B. software glitches
C. hurricanes
D. computer failures
E. floods
F. tornados
G. internal labor disputes
H. distributor troubles
I. fires
J. wars
K. riots
L. credit problems
M. government restrictions

➤ **Case Study**

In 2008, export company A in Sichuan of China signed a contract with a USA company, importing a piece of equipment. However, in May, there was an earthquake happened in Sichuan, where the exporter is. All the goods were destroyed in the earthquake; the exporter had to ask for the termination of the contract on the basis of force majeure event.

Is the exporter appropriate in asking for the termination? Why or why not?

4. Arbitration

When disputes arise between the seller and the buyer, there are four ways to *in sequence*: *negotiation, mediation, arbitration and litigation*[1].

Friendly negotiation and mediation are the most popular ways in the process of dispute settlement, which are able to *maintain friendship*[2] between the exporter and the importer. However, in practice, sometimes it is not very easy for the two sides to reach an agreement through friendly negotiation and mediation.

Then the two parties *turn to*[3] litigation and arbitration. Litigation means lawsuit, a process in law instituted by one party to *compel another to do him justice*[4]. It is usually costly and *time-consuming*[5]. Compared with litigation, arbitration may save both the cost and the time. Moreover, it will not *ruin the relation*[6] between the two sides and helps to preserve a long-term business relationship. Therefore, we are going to have a further introduction on arbitration.

Definition of Arbitration

Arbitration means a method of settling disputes arising between the two sides of parties who voluntarily render their disputes to a panel of arbitrators agreed by themselves[7] to deal with in accordance with certain arbitration rules and make a final decision binding both two parties based on the arbitration agreement the parties have reached.

Characteristics of Arbitration

◇ Voluntarily

The litigants submit themselves voluntarily to an arbitrator[8]. The arbitrator is *a private, disinterested person*[9], or nonofficial government organization chosen by the parties to a disputed question.

◇ An arbitration agreement

An arbitration agreement in written form between the parties concerned, which is *prerequisite for arbitration*[10]. Arbitration agreement can be made before or after disputes arise, which is a contract between two or more parties whereby they agree to refer the subject in dispute to others and to be bound by their award. Without it, the arbitration would *be groundless*[11].

◇ *Relative simplicity*[12]

Arbitration is simpler in procedures, less costly and time-consuming than litigation.

◇ The award is final and binding on both parties

Neither party may bring a suit before a law court or make a request to any other organization for revising the arbitral award[13]. But if one party refuses to *obey the award*, the other can ask a court to enforce the implementation of the award. The characteristic of finality of arbitral award is the basic element of the modern commercial arbitration recognized all over the world. Another situation is that, when the procedures of arbitration are discovered to be illegal, a lawsuit can be filed in respect of award of arbitration.

Arbitration Clauses

An arbitration clause in any import or export contract shall be regarded as existing independently and separately from the other clauses of the contract. It usually stipulates the arbitration body, the place of arbitration, the arbitration award, arbitration procedures and arbitration fees in the contract.

◇ The arbitration body

The arbitration body can be a temporary organized body for specific arbitration and which is dismissed when the arbitration is over, or *it may be a permanent arbitration body, such as the Arbitration Court of International Chamber of Commerce (ICC), the London Court of Arbitration, and American Arbitration Association and so on*[14].

In our country, *the China International Economic and Trade Arbitration Commission (CIETAC)*[15] in Beijing, and its chapters in Shenzhen and Shanghai, and offices in Dalian, Fuzhou, Changsha, Chengdu and Chongqing accept arbitration cases according to arbitration rules and regulations, and use the unified Arbitration Rules and Panel of Arbitrators.

◇ Place of arbitration

As we know, the place of arbitration will decide which arbitration rules or laws are applicable. Location is not only a matter of convenience. It is also related to the application of the law system under which the disputes are settled. The arbitration place can be anywhere in the seller's country, the buyer's country or a third country. The concerned parties always try to choose a place of arbitration they know well. The arbitration place is the first important place in recognition and enforcement of an arbitral award so it should be specified clearly in the arbitration agreement. Therefore, no matter where the arbitration takes place, the location must be politically and professionally acceptable.

◇ Arbitration award

An award is the decision made by *the arbitration tribunal*[16]. Once the award of arbitration is made, it is usually final and binding upon both parties. It must be in written form with or without explanations or reasons. If an arbitration clause doesn't conclude that the arbitral award is final, CIETAC will not accept the case.

◇ Arbitration procedures

Almost every permanent organization of arbitration has its own procedures of arbitration to deal with arbitration. In China, *pursuant to*[17] the rules of the main arbitration body, the China International Economic and Trade Arbitration Commission (CIETAC), the general arbitration procedure is as the following:
- Application for arbitration
- *Forming arbitration tribunal*[18]
- Hearing an arbitration case
- Issuing an award
- *Setting aside*[19] an award
- Enforcing an award

◇ Arbitration fees

It is sure that to arbitrate a dispute costs some. An arbitration agreement shall provide that which party is to *bear the arbitration fees*[20]. Generally, the arbitration clause shall provide that the arbitration fees shall be borne by *the losing party*[21]. Sometimes, it can be divided between be two parties or can be paid according to the award.

Arbitration Clause in Sales Contract

In order to settle the possible disputes smoothly and quickly, most parties previously conclude the arbitration clause in their contracts. Then any dispute related to the contract would submit to arbitration according to this clause. If no dispute arises through the transaction, the clause will not be used.

The following is an example of the arbitration clause in international trade contract:

"All disputes *in connection with*[22] the contract or the execution thereof shall be settled through friendly negotiations. In case no settlement can be reached through negotiations, the case should then be submitted for arbitration to the Foreign Trade Arbitration Commission of the China Council for the Promotion of International Trade. The decision rendered by the said Commission shall be final and binding upon both parties. The arbitration fee shall be borne by the losing party."

Notes

1. in sequence：negotiation，mediation，arbitration and litigation：依次为：协商、调解、仲裁和诉讼
2. maintain friendship：保持友好关系
3. turn to：求助于
4. compel another to do him justice：强迫另一方公平对待自己
5. time-consuming：浪费时间
6. ruin the relation：破坏关系
7. Arbitration means a method of settling disputes arising between the two sides of parties who voluntarily render their disputes to a panel of arbitrators agreed by themselves：仲裁指双方自愿把他们之间的争议交给双方都同意的仲裁机构进行裁决的一种解决争端的方式
8. The litigants submit themselves voluntarily to an arbitrator：诉讼当事人自愿提交给仲裁人
9. a private，disinterested person：一个单独的、公证的人
10. prerequisite for arbitration：仲裁的先决条件
11. be groundless：无理由、无根据的
12. relative simplicity：相对简单
13. Neither party may bring a suit before a law court or make a request to any other organization for revising the arbitral award：任何一方不能把有关争议案件提交法院审核，或者将仲裁决定向其他组织提出复审
14. It may be a permanent arbitration body，such as the Arbitration Court of International Chamber of Commerce（ICC），the London Court of Arbitration，and American Arbitration Association and so on：它可能是一个常设的仲裁机构，比如：国际商会仲裁院、伦敦国际仲裁院、美国仲裁协会等
15. the China International Economic and Trade Arbitration Commission（CIETAC）：中国国际经济贸易仲裁委员会
16. the arbitration tribunal：仲裁庭
17. pursuant to：依照；依据
18. forming arbitration tribunal：组成仲裁庭
19. setting aside：取消
20. bear the arbitration fees：承担仲裁费用
21. the losing party：败诉方

22. in connection with: 与……有关

 **In Practice**

➤ **Questions Based on the Text**

I. Decide whether the following statements are true or false according to the text.
1. Arbitration is the settling of a dispute by a person or persons chosen by the parties in controversy. ( )
2. Arbitration is simpler, less costly and time-consuming and more flexible than litigation. ( )
3. Arbitration agreement is agreed by both parties, which has to be made before disputes arise. ( )
4. The place of arbitration can be in the seller's country or the buyer's country, but it is not allowed in a third country. ( )
5. The arbitration award from a temporary arbitration tribunal can be asked for revising if one of the parties makes a request. ( )
6. If one party refuses to obey the award, the other can ask the other arbitration body to enforce the implementation of the award. ( )
7. An award is "final and binding" in China and most of the other countries provided that there are no illegal actions by any party involved in the arbitration process. ( )
8. An arbitration clause is part of the contract, but existing independently and separately from the other clauses of the contract. ( )

II. Answer these questions according to the text.
1. What is arbitration?
2. What will be included in an arbitration clause?
3. How many arbitration bodies do you know? Give their names.
4. What is the force of an arbitration award?
5. In most cases, who will bear the arbitration fee?

➤ **Business Vocabulary and Useful Expressions**

III. Translate the following terms.
1. negotiation and mediation _____

Chapter 8
Inspection, Claim, Force Majeure and Arbitration

2. ruin the relation _____
3. render the dispute _____
4. a permanent arbitration body _____
5. arbitration tribunal _____
6. pursuant to _____
7. 败诉方 _____
8. 与……有关的 _____
9. 承担仲裁费用 _____
10. 美国仲裁协会 _____
11. 仲裁裁定 _____
12. 强迫……公平对待 _____

IV. Fill in the blanks with words or phrases given below. Change the form where necessary.

> litigation   justice   voluntarily   disinterested   prerequisite

1. A journalist should always live up to the ideals of truth, decency and _____.
2. They will never _____ give up their independence.
3. The settlement ends more than four years of _____ on behalf of the residents.
4. Stability is a _____ for reform and development.
5. Every mother of their children in the small village are _____ and do everything for their children.

> groundless   illegal   independent   tribunal   unified

6. Scientists in different countries, working _____ of each other, have come up with very similar results.
7. I can say with confidence that such rumors were totally _____.
8. The _____ trade in animal products continues to flourish.
9. The arbitration _____ shall be entitled to require security for the costs of such measures.
10. _____ retail prices across the country will be worked out when feasible.

> in sequence   reach an agreement   compel to   pursuant to   in connection with

11. We cannot _____ you _____ help your sister, but we think you should.
12. _____ his instruction, I have placed an order for 10 cases of wine.

13. The numbers are not _____, they are all jumbled up.
14. If we want to _____ on the price, we will have to provide 5% discount.
15. Police are holding two men _____ last Thursday's bank robbery.

➢ Workshop

Arbitration is a dispute resolution mechanism. It is an alternative to litigating a case through the court system. A well-drafted arbitration provision usually addresses each of the following matters.

    A. The scope of the arbitration provision.
    B. Administration of the arbitration by the parties or an organization.
    C. The number of arbitrators to serve on the tribunal.
    D. The procedure for selecting the tribunal.
    E. The period within which the arbitration must begin.
    F. The choice of place.
    G. The choice of law.
    H. Enforcement of the arbitration award and appellate review.

Please read the arbitration clauses carefully and match some of the matters with the arbitration clauses:

1. The parties agree to submit to arbitration administered by the American Arbitration Association under its Commercial Arbitration Rules the following controversy.
    (   )

2. The arbitration is to be conducted before a single arbitrator whom the parties shall jointly select. If the parties are unable to agree upon the arbitrator, either party may request the American Arbitration Association to select the arbitrator. (   )

3. Any arbitration proceeding under this Agreement must be commenced no later than one year after the controversy or claim arises. Failure timely to commence an arbitration proceeding is both an absolute bar to the commencement of arbitration proceedings with respect to the controversy or claim and a waiver of the controversy or claim. (   )

4. In rendering an award, the arbitrator is to determine the rights and obligations of the parties according to the substantive and procedural laws of (state). (   )

5. The arbitration is to be conducted in New York. (   )

6. Each party shall submit to any court of competent jurisdiction for purposes of the enforcement of any award, order or judgment. Any award, order or judgment pursuant to arbitration is final and may be entered and enforced in any court of

competent jurisdiction. (   )

> **Case Study**

A Chinese company exported food products to Vietnam under L/C. The arbitration clause was made in the sales contract:

Any controversy or claim arising out of or relating to this Agreement or its breach, is to be settled by arbitration administered by the China International Economic and Trade Arbitration Commission (CIETAC) in accordance with commission's arbitration rules. The arbitration is to be conducted in Beijing and the arbitration award is final and binding upon both parties.

Due to bad quality, the buyer asked for arbitration in Vietnam in accordance with its rules. Is the request available?